# Internal Revolution

Be part of a Rising Generation

Rob Joy

When I first met Rob, he was a violent drug addict, just out of prison, who was gripped by intense fear. He stood opposed to God. I have seen first-hand how God has turned his life around. It has not always been an easy walk, but by God's power he has overcome the evil one and now stands as a powerful tool in God's hands. It is with pleasure and a great sense of triumph that I recommend this book and Rob's ministry.

*Pete McAllen, musician and worship pastor,*
*C3 Church, Cambridge*

Rob Joy is a genuine bloke. In this, his tell-it-as-it-is account of his life so far, you will get to know him pretty well. It's a bumpy ride in places, but you'll feel you're right there with him, a part of his amazing journey. This is a book you will pick up and not want to put down.

Rob is an all-or-nothing kind of guy, a real man of action. His energy is powerful, never failing to make an impact. Whether it's standing up for his mates, speaking out about what he believes, or exploiting a life of drugs and crime, there are no half measures. This story is full of high drama.

It's a fact of our modern world that a lot of people today are struggling in their lives, hurting, troubled and stuck in their own 'prison' or sense of hell on earth. That's especially true when it comes to addictions. Something that seems like a good idea for fun or thrills at the beginning can soon grip you, leaving you trapped, unable to break through. You'll see a lot of that and the trouble it brings in Rob's story, but you'll also come face to face with a stunning reality – things don't have to stay the way they are. Man, the world today sure needs to hear that from someone. Maybe you need to hear it too. Well, read on.

Maybe for you, reading this book will be like striking the match that injects a glimmer of light into your darkness, a ray of hope into your desperation. Or maybe it will help reinforce your fragile resolve to make the most of your life and escape the snare of your past or present lifestyle.

There's another group of people I would urge to read this book. In the midst of struggling humanity, there are those who have pushed through the demands on our time and our attention and have found fulfilment in helping others build and rebuild their lives. If that's you, this book will cheer you on. You'll see again that there really is hope and there really are answers.

Whatever the case, and wherever you're at right now, when you read Rob's story you'll be moved. I admit that I cried as I read it. Some tears of pain and some of joy.

Rob's a special guy, a real champion. I'm glad he's taken the plunge and written this down on paper for us. Read it, please. Your life, and maybe many others', will never be the same again.

*Mike Parkyn, former pastor, The Wave Church,*
*Hertfordshire, UK*

# Internal Revolution

**One man's incredible journey from near
death to new life**

Rob Joy

**Authentic**

Copyright © 2012 Rob Joy

18 17 16 15 14 13 12    7 6 5 4 3 2 1

First published 2012 by Authentic Media Limited
52 Presley Way, Crownhill, Milton Keynes, MK8 0ES
www.authenticmedia.co.uk

**British Library Cataloguing in Publication Data**

A catalogue record for this book is available from the
British Library

ISBN 978-1-86024-854-2

Scripture quotations are taken from the Holy Bible, Easy-to-Read
Version™ (Anglicized edition). Copyright © 2012 by Authentic
Media Limited. Used by permission. All rights reserved.

Some names in this book have been changed to protect identities.

Cover design by David Lund
Printed and Bound by CPI Group (UK) Ltd., Croydon, CR0 4YY

This book is dedicated to my darling son, Callum, the very hope I know God gave me to help escape the torment I was in – love you, son.

To everyone who is struggling with an addiction, homelessness, mental health issues or depression – pray that as you read my story, it will give you hope and set you free.

# Contents

# Acknowledgements

There are so many people I want to thank for helping me to make this book possible.

My praying mum and sisters: they never gave up, but believed in the promises God gave them for me. Thank you.

Pastors Mike and Heather Parkyn (and Claire and Michaela): you laid down your lives to help restore mine. You taught me the foundations of my Christian walk. I love you guys. Thank you.

Also, everyone from The Wave Church.

Pete and Ryan: you have been my inspirational and truly righteous brothers in Christ – 'Gosh!' Thank you for being there.

Ste and Sarah: your passion for the lost helped to fuel mine. Keep on fire, guys.

I want to include a special thanks to Guido, who has been and still is a massive encouragement to me. And everyone from 'Fire School' – keep doing it!

My good friend Rob, thanks for all you do for me, bro.

My best man and faithful friend, Corey.

Peter Johnson: you are a leader in your own right.

I am really grateful to the many people who have helped me put this book together: you have endured the endless editing and spent hours proofreading. To each and everyone of you – thank you.

A huge thank you to the team at Authentic Media for all their input and support, especially Malcolm Down for believing in the book.

Dominic and Jodi De Souza: for believing in me and giving me a platform to grow on.

My amazing wife Lydia, who shares my heart in all we do. I love you, baby.

A word of sincere thanks to all those who have been praying for me and encouraging me – individuals and churches. It has been a source of strength and enabled me to keep going. Let's reap a harvest!

Finally, the greatest thanks go to my Saviour, Jesus Christ, who gave his life for mine. He died in my place and gave me a second chance. I am really grateful.

Praise you.

# Foreword

I first met Rob when I was invited to speak at a conference run by his church in Letchworth. As a speaker, life is always so much easier for you when you stand in front of a crowd of people who you can see by the look on their faces are cheering you on. The worst kind of meetings are when people look completely apathetic. On this particular occasion, there was a guy on the front row who was totally into it and engaging with me on every point. In fact, he had such a magnetic enthusiasm that I found myself drawn to have a chat with him after the first session.

As a result, I stumbled across what I can only describe as an incredible and frankly miraculous story of transformation. I was so struck by Rob that I invited him there and then to speak at our national conference. A month or so later, I watched as he held hundreds of men in rapt attention as he described the story of his life. In some senses, the first part of his story is tragically familiar. A rapid descent into drug culture, petty crime leading to serious violence and, ultimately, time in prison. But unlike many others, the story doesn't end there or continue into a spiral of re-offending and years of struggle with addiction and crime to pay for the habit.

Rob discovered the key to living a full-on, drug-free life. More than that, what happened to him was so powerful that I do not recognize the man in the book when I talk to Rob. In fact, the Rob I meet in the book is nowhere to be found in the Rob of today. He is a living testimony that your past, no matter what has happened to you, does not need to govern your future. He is living proof that there is a road to total freedom and life to the full.

My recommendation to you is this: read the book, ask what it means to you, then get some copies for your mates. It may just change your life.

*Carl Beech, General Director, Christian Vision for Men*

# Introduction

Our nation is in a mess, with the crime rate, prison statistics and drug abuse at an all-time high.

I believe that the only answer to our nation's problems is Jesus Christ. It really is as simple as that. No other remedy, no other solution but the love, truth and power of Christ will ever bring our nation (or any nation, for that matter) back to being a God-centred and moral land again. My heart burns day and night to see the changes I so passionately believe are not only possible but are available to us all, if we will humble ourselves and pray.

Throughout this book I have purposely laid myself bare, with a brutal honesty that was not only extremely difficult to re-live and write about, but that I hope will be extremely challenging for readers. We cannot keep burying our heads in the sand and wishing this epidemic away. We have a crisis that is getting progressively worse with every generation. I have lost friends to drug addiction, and I have friends who are in and out of prison because they do not know how to get out of the vicious circle or how God can change them.

There are countless books and films that seem to glorify a gangster lifestyle, but they rarely reveal the true horror, devastation and emptiness that such a lifestyle brings. We also live in a day that writes off such hardened, violent and addicted men and women, labelling them hopeless and a waste of time and space. I beg to differ. I am living, walking proof that there is always hope, that there's always a turning point in a person's life. I passionately believe that the only way for this change is through a real revelation of the Most High God.

I have a young son who needs someone to fight for him; he needs a father who stands up against this epidemic and refuses to conform to the ways of this world.

I have learnt the hard way how empty, meaningless and deceitful a life of crime, immorality, violence and addiction really is. By writing this book I hope to do three things:

1. Reveal the truth about a life without Christ.
2. Reveal the truth about the love and grace of Christ.
3. Reveal the power of Christ to change and then empower anyone to live God's way.

I encourage you to read on with an open mind and heart, and then ask yourself this question:

Is God real?

Writing this book was very hard for me. I had to relive some things I would sooner forget. However, I also wept tears of incredible joy. This book is entirely true, no hype, no exaggeration for effect, but the real journey I have been on that has led me to this moment in my life where I can honestly say before God and people – I am simply not the same person I was.

In the Bible God says:

Look, I am making everything new.

(Revelation 21:5)

*Rob Joy*
*Summer 2011*

# 1

# Early Days

'Shane! No-oo! Get off him!' It was too late. Shane was a huge Alsatian and the tiny Jack Russell didn't stand a chance as Shane tore into him. We'd all been playing nicely on the green, when this stray dog had wandered onto our playing field. Before anyone could do anything, the poor unsuspecting animal had been ripped to pieces. I remember running to my house screaming.

The whole thing left me both shocked and distressed. But I also remember thinking that I would never let myself be like that Jack Russell. I would always be on guard and ready for any attack that came my way, regardless of how big my attacker was. And so I made the decision at a young age that I would always be a fighter; I would be one who would fight to the end.

## Jackmans Estate

Growing up on the Jackmans Estate in Letchworth, Hertfordshire, was a lot of fun. Despite its terrible reputation, I have many happy memories of playing on the green and getting up to no good. There was a large crowd of us most days after school, and we'd often play football, marbles or 'Ting Tang Tommy' (a type of hide-and-seek game which I used to love), but despite all the fun, you could always guarantee a few fights.

For as long as I can remember, the estate had had a bad name for drink and drugs, and we'd often see some of the older lads having a punch-up. It wasn't very long before I started getting involved, too. Being shorter than most of the other lads only fuelled my anger and made me even more determined not to be pushed around. I'd always give as good as I got. The fights were never anything serious, though. A cut lip here, a black eye there – nothing to get excited about. All in all, though, I loved the Jackmans. I had plenty of good mates, and the older lads looked after us – they used to date my two older sisters, so I always felt protected.

One of the most exciting things for me was playing up the shops. We'd kick balls about or shout abuse at the locals and run off laughing. But what I really loved was watching the older lot going in and out of the local pub. I used to stare through the smudged windows, into the smoky atmosphere, watching them all drinking and playing pool. I used to imagine myself being there, pint in one hand, pool cue in the other. I couldn't wait to be older. Playing games paled in comparison whenever I thought of the pub scene. To be 'one of the lads' seemed like a dream back then, and whenever one of the locals came out and said hello, I'd feel six feet tall.

The highlight of my week had to be the Monday night disco. The entry fee was only 10p, and my friends and I would turn up dressed as cool as we could for 10-year-olds. With girls there it was inevitable that eventually we'd start showing off. We'd run around doing the stupidest, craziest stuff, just trying to impress them. A smile from a pretty girl was our pay-off.

## My Father, My Hero

The Jackmans had a community centre that my dad often took me to. I spent most weekends there, playing pool and causing some sort of trouble. Once I started to get good at pool, my old man taught me how to 'hustle'. Purposefully missing shots, I'd wait for some unlucky punter to notice. Then after my dad convinced them to play me for a quid or so, I'd turn up the heat and end up pocketing the money. It all seemed pretty harmless and I was a quick learner. I'll never forget my dad first teaching me how to 'earn' money.

I loved my dad dearly and I'm sure he loved me too, but our relationship was very up and down. My two older sisters were from my mum's first marriage, so inevitably I became my dad's pride and joy. In my eyes he was great and, like most kids, I guess, I wanted to be just like him.

Dad was a recovering alcoholic. After many years of alcohol abuse, he finally gave it up after I was born. People have told me the story of how Dad went out to wet the baby's head. Now for most people this would take a few hours at most, but my dad dragged it out for three weeks. After a few more months of this, Mum had no choice but to put her foot down. However, when I was about 9 months old my dad made a firm decision to put me before the booze after turning up completely off his face at his drinking partner's house. At that point he vowed, 'This is it. I have a baby boy and I'll never let him see me drunk.' I never did.

My mum managed to get him into rehab at the local hospital. At first they wouldn't take him, so my mum started getting hysterical, ripping posters off the walls and making a real scene. Thankfully, after a while they took him in, and helped him to get dry.

I'd hear that story and think how great my dad was, doing all that for me. He was my hero. Unfortunately, the years of drinking and heavy smoking had taken their toll on his health, so I missed out on the stuff the other dads were doing with their kids, such as playing football. Dad tried to show his affection in other ways – one being, he bought me things. He'd come home with sweets and toys and was always very generous with his money. He wasn't the type to show his emotions and, although I'm sure he probably did, I have no memory of him cuddling me or telling me he loved me. Being a young kid, I wasn't going to complain; I just accepted that this was the way he was.

I was frequently left disappointed, though, by his broken promises. I would beg Dad to play football with me or take me somewhere – and he would promise to, often swearing on his life that he would take me 'tomorrow'. But tomorrow never came. I can remember being gutted every time. I'd often cry myself to sleep over this but I made sure Dad never heard me, because he told me that crying was for the weak. The next day my dad would stroll into my room, throw me a new toy or a pack of sweets, apologize for letting me down and then promise me all over again. I'm not looking for sympathy here. That's just the way it was.

My dad was great at other stuff – like stopping my mum from whacking me. She was the one who disciplined me – when my dad let her. If she tried to hit me, he'd pick me up and shield me from her wild swings. I'd soon forget about the broken promises after he had defended me from my raging mum. Yeah, he was great, my dad!

When I was about 9, I was told we were moving house. I couldn't believe it. I didn't want to move. I loved the Jackmans and the green and the shops and all my mates, and we were moving what seemed like miles away – it was actually just a five-minute walk away, but I didn't see it that way.

However, I soon changed my mind when I saw the house. It was a lot bigger, and the back garden was massive. I started to plan a tree house and different things before we'd even moved in. I was very excited. I made friends with the kids over the road, a really nice black family; some of the kids even went to my school. It was all getting better and better for me.

My new house had a big garage as well, which I turned into a bit of a den. We'd get up to all sorts of things in there, mostly kick boxing training. I'd charge the other kids a pound to join my classes. To tell you the truth, I'd never even been to a kick boxing class, or anything like that – I used to watch a lot of Jackie Chan and Jean-Claude Van Damme films, so I felt I was a bit of an expert.

## School Days

When I was 11, I joined Highfield Secondary School and started to develop a real attitude, influenced by the *Karate Kid* films and *Hong Kong Phooey* cartoons. I tried out my moves on the other kids and got into loads of trouble. Me and some friends were walking through the town once after school and I wanted to show off a new move I'd learnt, so I bet the others I could walk up to the tall kid in front of us and take him out in one move. This got them all going and I was egged on in my mission. I approached this poor lad, who had done absolutely nothing wrong, and tapped him on the shoulder. As he turned around I knocked him to the ground with a flying kick to his face. We all ran off laughing. My reputation had kicked off.

Not long after that, the head teacher at Highfield and my mum agreed that it would be best for everyone if I moved to another school. I soon found myself walking through the gates of Knights Templar School in nearby Baldock. I joined them in the second year and, as I already knew a few kids who went there, I settled in nicely. I was given a very strict warning by my new headmaster that if anything of my reputation followed me, I'd be straight out. What a challenge I had been set! I absolutely terrorized that poor school. I broke records for the most suspensions in the school's history, I gave one teacher a nervous breakdown, and I caused many others to go grey well before their time. I found it all hilarious.

By about the third year I was becoming a real 'Del Boy' (a wheeler-dealer, like the fictional character in *Only Fools and Horses*). My dad often had boxes of fake designer clothes, aftershaves, watches and kids' videos. He would buy everything and anything that he could make a profit on, and I was no different. I was always in the playground with a crowd around me, doing my sales pitch (Dad was a great teacher). I once even conned a fifth-former into buying a French cigarette for £2 – I told him it was a joint. The same lad came looking for me later on, and I thought he wanted to beat me up. How I laughed when instead he asked me if I could get any more. 'It was the best joint I've ever had,' he said.

Things started to get really bad at home, though, and I hated the constant rows between my mum and dad. Mum, by this time, had become a devout Christian. She had turned her back on the pub scene and had given up her shoplifting habit. She continually went on about how great Jesus was and how amazing God was. Dad found this all too much and would really 'kick off' about her new religion. I regularly cried myself to sleep, hearing them screaming at each other. The rows got worse and worse and I started to punch walls and cut my arms as a way of relieving some of the stress I was feeling.

For a while I had enjoyed going to church with Mum, but Dad put a stop to all that. He would call Christians 'nutters' and say they were brainwashed. Anyway, I wanted to be like my dad, so I eventually started copying whatever he said. I'd call my mum all sorts of names and became very abusive towards her. My parents separated on a few occasions, and I was over the moon when Mum moved out and it was just me and Dad. But they always got back together again. My dad just could not cope without Mum and he put on the charm, promised her the world, and she soon returned home.

This went on for years and it took its toll on me. I began to hate religion with a passion. It had caused such division in my family. I became a clone of my dad. Although he was a great man in many ways, he could be nasty in others and was emotionally scarred from his own upbringing. He was racially prejudiced towards my sisters' black boyfriends – the abuse that came out of his mouth at times was horrible. I had black friends myself, and often got very upset with him, but after a while I gave in and started copying my dad. I had become a fake racist.

As I look back at my home life I have mixed feelings. It could be like a battlefield a lot of the time, but despite this there was no denying the fact that my parents really did love each other. We had some good times as a family, and I was very lucky to get a holiday abroad every year. If you looked through some of our family albums, they would probably tell a story of a close family and belied the reality of the constant rows and tension which stained those memories for me.

# 2

# A Big Mistake

My school days came to end and, having not even bothered with my exams, it came as no surprise when I got my results. I got mostly As (which stood for 'absent'). But what did I care? My dad had his own roofing company and I walked straight into a job.

I loved roofing and enjoyed getting stuck in to a day's work. Granted, I wasn't very clever when it came to working stuff out, but show me a pallet of tiles that needed to go up and I'd have them on the roof in no time.

Today I can see that going to work for my dad was one of the biggest mistakes I ever made. We started to argue a lot more at work and this made home life even more tense. A lot of this was down to my 'secret' heavy drinking.

## The Main Boyz

During my school days I had spent a lot of time hanging around the local snooker club, which was where I met Rick, who was to become my best friend. He was the same age as me and had moved down to Letchworth from Glasgow. We started playing a lot of snooker together and we both became very good players. We often spent hours at a time practising and hanging out at the snooker club. My dad would give us both some spending money, and when the money ran out, the owner let us collect glasses and wipe the counters down to earn ourselves a couple of pints.

I grew to really enjoy my beer, and Rick and I got into some terrible states. My mum once found us both so drunk that she slapped me round the face and I didn't feel a thing. There was also the time I ended up in hospital with alcohol poisoning. I was about 14.

Rick and I were inseparable. We went everywhere together and got up to all sorts of dodgy stuff. We ended up living together, and we nearly ended up dying together as well.

We'd met up and become very good friends with another two lads called Matt and Jon. We had met them at the snooker club, and the four of us were deadly, always drinking and fighting and taking the mickey out of anyone who came near us. Then Jamie joined us and we formed a little gang called the 'Five Main Boyz'. We were only 16. Each of us even went as far as getting a Main Boyz tattoo, which has provided me with a permanent reminder of just how daft we were.

One night while we were having a few beers at a local pub, a group of lads walked into the garden area where we were sitting. They were some of my old Jackmans friends. I hadn't seen them in ages, but I'd been hearing quite a lot about them always fighting in the pubs and getting in trouble. As you can imagine, I was thrilled to see them, and the Five Main Boyz combined with the Jackmans Boyz quite nicely. Now the fun really began. There were roughly twenty-five of us altogether and we became quite a force to be reckoned with.

We made our way from pub to pub causing trouble wherever we went and developed a bad reputation for ourselves. Even though we were all between 16 and 17, it never stopped us taking on anyone and everyone. We soon ran out of competition of our own age and moved on to the next level – bouncers and other groups of older lads. We really didn't care. If one 'kicked off' the others 'kicked off' – that's just how it was. There was no stopping us.

## Acquiring a Taste

In the summer of 1996 we made our way to a new pub in Baldock, all twenty-five of us. The look on the doormen's faces when we walked in was a picture. They'd heard all about us but it was obvious they weren't going to say anything, so in we went. As usual we found a corner of the pub and took it over. We all stuck together. If one of us went to buy a drink, he'd be followed by a couple of the others, just in case someone 'tried it on' while he was alone. This was my way of life for the next ten years.

It was while drinking in this pub in 1996 that I tried my first drug. A friend of mine offered it to me to help sober me up. I'd been drinking heavily and, as usual, wanted to fight the world. Reluctantly, I took the dab of speed (amphetamine) he gave me, and my mood instantly changed from being really aggressive to really happy. The people I'd wanted to beat up suddenly became my friends! I had the best night I'd ever had and I thought, *Wow, if this is all it takes to give me a great night, and stop me being so 'aggro', I'll take some more often – only a little bit, though, 'cos I don't wanna become addict-ed*. That was the biggest mistake I've ever made.

I became a regular user of speed, and the amount I had to take to get the same effect became greater and greater. At first I only took it on Friday nights, then it was Fridays and Saturdays but within a month or two I was taking it every day. It seemed to happen overnight, but very soon I was totally dependent on this drug. I started buying more and more, and start-ed supplying all my friends. Before long I was the largest supplier of top-class base speed in the area. My friends and I took outrageous amounts of the stuff to stay high, sometimes going for days without sleep or food.

Things started to get really bad when a new pub opened in Letchworth. On the opening night we went in there mob-handed, and we loved it. This pub was right up our street. The doormen seemed OK and they left us alone to do what we had to do.

One Friday night, one of the bouncers approached me and said he'd heard I was the local dealer and I'd been selling drugs in the pub. I told him he had heard right and that I wasn't going to stop, either. So we came to a mutual agreement that the doormen would leave me and the lads to do what we wanted if we cut them in on the deal.

I'd only been selling speed at this point, but I had tried a few lines of coke (cocaine) over the past few weeks. This bouncer offered to bring me some top gear from London every Friday night, if I'd give him a cut of the profits. I took him up on his offer and the following week, as arranged, I came to the pub and let him search me very dramatically in front of the manager. We then went straight up the stairs to the toilets where he had stashed loads of wraps of coke, base speed and a few Es (Ecstasy tablets).

So it began. I'd pass the gear over to a couple of my mates after I'd taken a nice fat gram for myself, and they'd go around selling the stuff for me. I would stand in my usual place, drinking and chatting away, and when anyone asked me for some gear, I'd take the money from them and then point out the guy I had holding the stuff. I never kept the money and the drugs on me at the same time as it was far too risky.

I'd always pay someone else to hold the drugs for me. At the end of the night I'd leave whatever money I had to for the bouncer, and still have a couple of hundred left for myself, as well as a load of 'percy' (personal drugs). Then we'd all go back to my room.

By that time I had been kicked out of home for being disrespectful to my mum and I was renting a room in one of my dad's other houses. My dad had bought two other properties to rent out as bedsits and I was allowed to move into one of the rooms. On a good night I might have up to thirty people in this one room all drinking and sticking their fingers into a bag of my speed – although I and one or two of the others had progressed onto cocaine full-time by now. Coke was a lot more expensive and the effects didn't last as long, but the buzz was a lot greater.

## Big Mac Brawl

The drugs very quickly changed my personality. I became increasingly violent and edgy. When we were all in the pub I was OK, but I started to imagine that one of my many enemies would try to kill me when I wasn't looking. If I went to the toilet I'd have someone follow me and wait next to me in case anyone tried it on. One night, however, my suspicions were proved right.

We were all out at the pub, drinking and being aggressive, when I noticed that my mate Liam was arguing with a couple of Asian lads. I flew over and told them to 'get lost' if they wanted to go home that night. They got the idea and left, so we carried on drinking until chucking-out time. After a while we regrouped and me and the Boyz made our way to McDonald's for some food, with the intention of continuing the night back at my place.

About eight of us were sitting down eating, when the two Asian lads walked in, followed by another three shortly afterwards. Well, it didn't take a rocket scientist to work out that they weren't coming in for a McFlurry. Liam stood up and stormed over to confront them. I was directly behind him.

I had got into the habit of carrying some sort of weapon whenever I was out. On this occasion I had a rugby sock filled with wet sand, tied with a knot to stop it spilling out. My dad had caught me the previous week with a sock containing two huge ball bearings. He'd warned me that I'd kill someone if I hit them with it. I hadn't really considered that, and reluctantly agreed to use wet sand instead – he told me he used to use this and it did the job.

Within seconds of both sides squaring up, one of the Asian lads threw the first punch. It landed on my mate Alan, which was probably the worst thing the Asian lad could have done. Alan was a talented boxer and a seriously 'hard' bloke. He didn't hesitate and went straight into action on this guy. I decided to help out by swinging my weapon as hard as I could, and got stuck in to the huge brawl that had now erupted.

We had all piled in by now, as had the Asian lads, and the scene was looking very ugly. Innocent bystanders were getting hit as chairs went flying. The Asian guys were taking a serious beating. The shocked manageress panicked and decided to lock the doors so that no one else could get in, but that meant that none of us could get out either. Fists continued to fly for some time, and in the chaos I shouted at one of the staff to get the doors open. Once they were opened, we all made it outside seconds before the police arrived. Not wanting to get caught with a weapon on me, I threw the sock into a shop doorway and walked calmly past the police.

To our amazement we all got away without being arrested and headed back to my place to reflect on what had just happened. I knew it was bad, but I didn't realize just how bad until the next day.

## Caught on Camera

The police taped off the whole area and forensics were taking fingerprints and studying the weapon they had found in a shop doorway. The Asian lads were in a bad way. We were told by a friend that it didn't look very good for one of them in particular. He had suffered serious injuries including a fractured skull, a shattered cheekbone, multiple gashes and facial bruising. The whole incident had caused his epilepsy to return. He was now in a coma and the police were gunning for us all. I still remember coldly saying to my dad that I didn't care, and that if he died, he died. Looking back, it was all about me trying to look like the gangster I aspired to be.

It didn't take long for the police to catch up with us, and before long we were all arrested and charged. We were bailed to appear at court charged with GBH (grievous bodily harm), ABH (actual bodily harm) and violent disorder. Unfortunately, I had an extra charge for my use of an offensive weapon. It probably didn't do us any favours when the local papers got wind of what had happened. They had a field day with the story.

Normally I would never have pleaded guilty, but due to the overwhelming evidence against me as a result of the CCTV footage, I didn't have much choice. They had me clearly on camera, pulling out the sock filled with wet sand and hitting one of the Asian guys in the face with it. Moreover, there were loads of eye-witness statements, including the staff at McDonald's, who all knew of me.

I was bailed with the other lads and told to return to court for sentencing. Being the only one who had pleaded guilty, I was given loads of bail conditions. I was told to leave Hertfordshire and I was told I wasn't allowed to enter any licensed premises in the entire UK (which I'm sure must be some sort of record). I had to sign on at the local police station when I moved to the neighbouring county of Bedfordshire, and they gave me a curfew.

My dad had arranged for me to stay at one of his roofers' houses. He sent me off with some cash, a few clothes and a case of beer. When I got there, I began to reflect for the first time on the trouble I was in. But I very quickly forgot all about it when I met Leanne, the roofer's stepdaughter. She was gorgeous. We started seeing each other and became very close, which was a very bad idea, as I only had a couple of months to go before sentencing.

The day of the court case arrived and I looked a mess. The night before, one of my friends had had a party back in Baldock and they had wanted me to be there. So they sent someone to pick me up and sneak me in the back door of this little club they were all in. Needless to say the drugs came out and I started downing vodka. The alcohol only fuelled my already unstable emotions and I started to get angry at the thought of being sent away from all my mates. In my anger I smashed an ashtray and stupidly carved NF into my right arm. It serves as another constant reminder of just how ignorant and stupid I was in those days.

When I got back to Bedford and sobered up, I realized just what I'd done. I was about to go in for sentencing for racially aggravated assault with a skinhead haircut, wearing black combat trousers and a white Ben Sherman shirt and, as if that wasn't bad enough, I now had a racist slogan carved into my arm. The only thing I could think to do was to get Leanne's brother to heat a sharp knife over the cooker and cut me again to try to disguise the letters. What a fool I had become.

At the time the Stephen Lawrence case in London was still fresh in people's minds. You're probably familiar with it if you read the newspapers – Stephen was the young black lad who was killed by a group of white kids in a racist attack.

There were rumours flying around that there was going to be a revenge attack at court, so we made sure a lot of our guys were present. My dad had arranged for a couple of his friends to be there as well, just in case, but thankfully nothing happened.

## Sentencing

The clerk called out our names and we made our way into the dock. We had gone through the trial and were waiting for a verdict; I was just waiting to be told how long I had to be away from my family and friends. One by one the verdicts came in. One was found not guilty (which was fair) but the rest of us were found guilty. Two got non-custodial sentences and the remaining five of us were given prison sentences.

After being told to expect a minimum of three years by my barrister I was very pleased when I was told eighteen months by the judge. However, I was surprised at Alan's sentence. He ended up getting two years, and he had one less charge than me. The judge said that because he was a boxer, his hands were classed as weapons. Alan was fuming and 'kicked off' down in the holding cells below the court. He eventually calmed down, and we all sat and waited for the Group 4 security van to come and drive us to our 'new homes'.

# 3

# Inside

When we all arrived at HMP Woodhill, I thought they were having a laugh. The place was like something out of an American film. It was an A Category (maximum security) prison. The angry-looking prison officer at reception set the scene nicely and was a sign of things to come. I remember thinking, *If this is what the 'screws' look like, then what are the cons going to be like?* Well, I soon found out.

After we spent about two hours being processed into the system, we were given a medical. Then we were led out into a huge yard where the armed guards and ferocious-looking Alsatian dogs were patrolling. I'm telling you, these animals could bark, and they were vicious as well.

As I looked around, I thought it all seemed a bit over the top. There were huge walls covered in barbed wire, and wire netting suspended above the whole yard to stop any helicopters from landing to break someone out. Honestly, this place wasn't taking any chances. It was not surprising, though, as I later found out it was the home of the infamous convict 'Charlie Bronson'. He was considered so dangerous that he was in a prison within the prison. He had only been sentenced to seven years, but had become so violent and unpredictable that they couldn't risk releasing him. He'd taken hostages and attacked prison guards. So all in all, it looked like I was in for a good time.

I was led onto the young offenders' wing, which was for people who were under the age of 21 – like me – and was shown to my cell on the ground floor. As the big metal door was slammed behind me, I looked around at my tiny 8 ft by 7 ft cell, which consisted of a rickety old bed, a filthy-looking toilet and sink, and a small table covered in chewing-gum – and other stuff.

I laughed out loud and shouted to Alan, who was in the cell next to mine: 'Welcome to the Ritz, bruv!' But however hard we tried to make a bad situation seem OK, the reality was that this place really was nothing to joke about.

I began to unpack my bag, which held some ill-fitting prison clothes with 'HMP WOODHILL' printed all over them in capital letters – 'What do they think we're gonna do,' I muttered, 'pinch them or something?' – and some tattered old plimsolls, which had me in hysterics. We used to call them 'Filas', because you used to 'fila (feel a) right idiot' when you wore them.

I had taken a few personal belongings to court with me – some of my own clothes, and so on – but I was told I'd get them back when I left. Honestly, what with these ridiculous plimsolls on my feet and a baggy red prison tracksuit, I must have looked like Coco the Clown. But I soon realized that it didn't matter. It wasn't as if I had anyone to impress in this place.

## Settling In

The first night was a bit hard. Everyone wanted to know where I was from and what I was in for, and all I wanted to do was lie on my bed and work out what went wrong. But I soon gave in to the shouts from other cells:

'Oi! Cell 11! What's ya name?'

'Rob.'

'Oi! Cell 11! What ya in for?'

'Beating someone up.'

'Oi! Cell 11! Swing us a burn on a line.'

'*What?*'

It turned out that a burn was a roll-up cigarette, and a line was something you made out of your bed sheets. You tied a bag with the burn in it on the end of your line and leant your arm out of the window between the bars, then the guy in the cell next to you would hold out his toilet brush as far as he could, and you would have to swing this makeshift line over his brush. He could then reel it in and collect the burn, or whatever else you were passing. I soon became an expert at this line-swinging. I actually found it quite amusing when I looked out of my cell window and saw the guy in cell 24 trying to reach the guy in cell 57 with a line that must have taken his entire bed sheet to make. After about a thousand swings, you'd hear them rejoicing when cell 57 had eventually caught this line and had successfully reeled in the bag – which probably just had a stamp in it, or something like that. Why they never waited until the morning and just gave the stuff to each other I don't know, but this wasn't normal life so I just tried to get on with it.

After a few days we had all settled in. Inside, we were just the same as we were on the outside. We stuck together everywhere we went, and when we were in the exercise yard, we all sat in our little corner or walked round and round the square yard together.

Our wing was actually alright. We had two pool tables and a table tennis table that we could use while we were on 'association'. But, as you can imagine, with about sixty lads all waiting, it was a bit of a nightmare getting a table.

The thing with prison is you never know what's going to happen from one day to the next. You could be best mates with someone one week and end up threatening to kill them the next. Emotions were always running high and you could always guarantee a good scrap during 'association' to liven things up a bit.

## Left Behind

After a couple of weeks or so, my mates Alan, Liam and Craig were suddenly shipped off to HMP/YOI Onley, a young offenders' institution in Rugby. Danny and I stayed put. That was a bit of a shock to the system, seeing three of the lads move on, but when I started moaning to the officers I was told that there wasn't an awful lot I could do about it.

Danny and I were put into a double cell together. It was OK, apart from the fact that the cell was the same size as the single cells except with bunk beds, so it wasn't long before we were getting on each other's nerves. Now me and Danny were very good pals, but it's amazing how much you can annoy someone when you're spending up to twenty hours a day in the same shoebox. Apart from that, though, we still kept a firm eye on each other's backs and if one of us found himself in trouble, the other was right there in the thick of it.

Then, completely out of the blue, just as we were getting used to the other boys being sent to another prison, our cell door was flung open early one morning and we were told to get our stuff together for a move. *Fantastic*, I thought, we*'re going to be reunited with the lads at Onley*. How wrong I was! We were chucked in a filthy old prison security van and were told at the last minute that we were on our way to HMP Norwich.

I can remember how upset I felt when I was told. I'd heard a few reports about this prison and they weren't very encouraging. After a few hours in this smelly old van, we were relieved when the driver told us we were pulling over for some lunch. I wasn't stupid enough to think we were stopping at a Little Chef, but when they pulled into the holding cells at Peterborough and gave us a stale crisp sandwich each, I started to get annoyed. By now I was beginning to understand that all the complaining in the world wasn't going to change the fact that I had next to no rights, and the prison officers didn't care one bit if Danny and I weren't happy with the service.

We finished the long haul to HMP Norwich and found ourselves looking through the windows at this old-style prison, which reminded me of the Ronnie Barker TV sitcom *Porridge*. This place took all the wind out of my sails. I thought at the time that it was like looking into the jaws of hell. This prison was nothing like Woodhill. It was dirty, rundown and practically medieval. I put on my tough face, although in truth I really just wanted to cry, and we made our way to the booking-in hall.

Danny and I were put into a really old double cell, with the same luxuries as our last one. As I write, I believe this is where I lost what little sanity I had left – it was during those three weeks I spent in Norwich. I was banged up in this cell with Danny for 23½ hours a day. We were only allowed out for fifteen minutes at lunch time and fifteen minutes at tea time to collect our disgusting prison food. After just two days there I was losing the plot. We spent hours putting ourselves through gruelling exercise routines in the cell – press-ups, sit-ups, squat thrusts, and anything else we could think of to keep ourselves fit and active. But it wasn't long before the pair of us wanted to throttle each other. Danny and I were really close but were very similar in our attitudes and that often caused us to clash.

Aside from the strict exercise programme, I spent a lot of my time writing letters. I used to really enjoy writing to the boys on the outside and keeping up to date with the action, as well as telling them all about our adventures inside. I also wrote to the lads in the other jail and compared the prisons and the food and so on. But I spent most of my time writing to Leanne.

We had become very close when I had stayed at her house on bail and we kept in regular contact now. It was the highlight of my week when one of her letters was posted under my door. I'd rip it open and read it several times, and she even got into the habit of spraying it with her perfume for me. (Amazing how soppy you can get after a few weeks locked up!) In all honesty, it was those letters and the odd phone call to someone outside that kept me from going totally crazy.

'LEWIS! Pack your bags,' said the screw. 'You're moving to Onley.'

## Moving On

Danny was well pleased. He was going to join the others at the 'holiday camp' – they had told us how luxurious it was there. Although I was pleased for him, I was gutted that I had to wait another week until I was moved to Onley too. Still, the week flew by thanks to some hardcore letter-writing and thousands of press-ups.

By the time I arrived at HMP/YOI Onley, I was getting hardened to it all and I walked through the gates into my new home with a much bigger chip on my shoulder than when I'd first been sentenced. I spent about three weeks on the induction wing before being moved onto A Wing, where I was reunited with Danny. Alan and Liam were on C Wing and Craig was over on E Wing, which was for people who had made a good impression on the governors and were allowed extra privileges.

A Wing was full of hormonal, angry and violent young men. It was a predominantly black wing and they didn't take too kindly to me and big Danny, a couple of neo-Nazi-looking white boys with serious attitude problems. But after a few days, the heat died down and we ended up making friends with a couple of interesting and very useful north London guys.

In Onley you had to work – either in one of the workshops doing bricklaying or carpentry and so on, or cleaning the wing or preparing the food for meal times. This could earn you up to £10.00 per week on top of the £10.00 per week you could have sent in privately, which my dad always did. This was meant to be spent on your canteen sheet which came round once a week, on which you were able to order treats such as toiletries, phone cards, tobacco and various types of snack food to keep you going in between the paltry portions of food they gave us.

However, the majority of the inmates didn't use the system as it was intended. They used their earnings to buy drugs. It was mostly spent on weed (cannabis), although there was a fair amount of heroin available inside. I have to confess, although I wasn't much of a smoker, I would occasionally trade one of my phone cards to buy a joint to help me sleep. It wasn't very often, though, because I loved ringing Leanne and people back home. I'd encourage them to send me a reply to my last letter so I could write another.

The most exciting time inside for me was visit day. You were allowed three visits per month and I'd spend ages trying to work out who I could see next, what with all the lads and my family as well. Arranging a visit was quite a stressful ordeal. I'd send out my VO (visiting order) and then spend the next few days chasing up the visitor to make sure they'd booked it. Then I'd be panicking on the day in case they were late, or worse still, that I'd get 'ghosted', which is when visitors don't show up at all.

I'd always panic over nothing on visiting day. My name was always called out and I'd march into the visiting room with my 'trendy' striped shirt on, which I always made sure was too small for me, so that my visitors could see how much I was bulking up from my weight training. Visits normally lasted about an hour. I'd cram in as much chat as I could without letting my visitor get a word in. Then, without fail, just before it was time for them to leave, out would come my threats: 'Make sure you tell everyone to write to me. Make sure you lot don't forget about us boys in here, and make sure you tell Martin he's dead when I get out.'

Martin had been a friend of ours, but he had done the unforgivable. He had grassed on one of his own. He and Danny had been involved in a fight just before we all got sentenced and, due to Martin's statement, Danny had ended up getting an extra eighteen months on his sentence. I was fuming. I'd lie in bed every night imagining ways I'd pay him back for ratting on my mate. This became an obsession and I'd regularly swear to Danny that I'd take care of it when I was released.

I ended up getting the best job in the prison – 'Gym Orderly'. This was my other obsession. I would train five or six days a week, eating everything I could and reading as many body-building magazines as possible. I loved training. I had the sort of genetic make-up that most weight lifters would love to have and I grew in size very quickly. The gym sessions were the main times we lads could meet up, as we were on different wings. We'd joke around, sharing stories and winding each other up.

The months seemed to go quite quickly in Onley, and it wasn't long before my release day was due. I was buzzing. The lads on the outside had arranged to pick me up in a stretch limo. After completing an additional seven days for a minor incident, I was ready to leave my prison life behind me and get back into the swing of things on the outside. But things didn't turn out quite as I had hoped.

# 4

# Revenge

I stepped outside of the huge iron gates and, with my prison bag slung over my shoulder, I made my way to the top of the road where I was to meet the boys. Within a few minutes I watched the stretch limo pull up next to me. Fifteen of my closest pals all piled out onto the grass verge and took it in turns to hug me and fire loads of questions at me.

It felt so good to see them and be back with them. I was overwhelmed by the whole thing and when I was finally bundled into the back of this limo, I was introduced to my first can of beer and line of coke in nine months. The fact that it was 9 a.m. didn't bother us. We had a lot of celebrating to do.

I can't really remember much about the journey except that everything seemed to go so fast. Although I hadn't spent a long time inside, it really does slow you down, and when you are doing 60 mph down the motorway in a stretch limo, surrounded by very boisterous mates, and under the influence of drink and drugs, it plays with your head a bit.

By the time I got to the probation office in Stevenage, I wasn't in the best state, but as usual I managed to blag my way through it. I signed the papers agreeing to stick to the terms of my release. Then I was free to go. The terms were that for the next nine months I had to report regularly to my probation officer and stay well away from trouble. I was under prison licence, which meant that if I as much as blew my nose the wrong way, I would go back inside.

## Getting Even

When I got back to Letchworth, I couldn't wait to meet all the others. They had arranged for a bit of a party to be held at one of the pubs in town. Everyone was going to be there. I went to my parents' house just for long enough to throw my bag in and say hello to Mum and Dad. My dad was more surprised than my mum to see how much I had grown. Mum had visited me a lot in jail, but my dad had only come once. I don't think he could handle it very well. Anyway, once I had got changed into my best clothes and put on a splash of aftershave, I was off into town.

The boys never left my side and I didn't have to put my hand in my pocket – the drinks were flowing, and so were the drugs. It didn't take very long before I was half-drunk and high as a kite. My dad arrived with a mate of his and they both cheered me up even more. They said they were going to pay for Leanne and her friend to get a taxi from Bedford to come to see me.

Leanne knew I was no angel, but I'm not sure she knew how bad I could be. When she and her friend arrived I was already quite drunk, but things got worse when we all decided we'd had enough of this pub and headed off for another. I think we'd only been there for about an hour when the trouble started. Jamie, Leanne, her friend and I were sitting quietly at a table, drinking, when Jamie noticed Martin walking past outside. Now, I'd made a promise to Danny and I wasn't about to forget it. I ran out of the pub armed with an empty beer bottle and gave chase. Luckily for him I was in no state to catch anyone, and after a few yards gave up and just threw the bottle at him. I went back to the pub and carried on drinking with Leanne and the others.

The following Wednesday I found myself in a nightclub in Stevenage with my best friend, Rick, and a few girls. On Wednesday nights the drinks were really cheap and it was eighties night. I loved having a dance to the eighties classics and getting smashed on cheap beer and vodka. Vodka was always my real poison, in the sense that it just didn't agree with me. I was usually OK if I stayed on the beer, but after too many I'd often hit the vodka and that spelt trouble. Whenever I went to drink it, the girls that we hung around with tried to talk me out of it and remind me what I could be like on it. This night, however, I wouldn't be told and I hit it hard.

I remember the night well, which is unusual, but no doubt has something to do with the way it ended. After a few pints and several vodkas, I made a quick visit to the toilet to 'powder my nose'. I rarely went on a night out without at least half a gram of 'sniff' (coke) and this night was no different.

I walked back out onto the dance floor and my mood very quickly changed. I'd been having a great night, good music, good company, enjoying the fact that I was free, but suddenly I remembered that my good friend Danny wasn't. He was still banged up because of that grass, Martin, and here I was, enjoying myself. I started to lose it and told Rick that I was off.

'Where to? The night's only young, bruv,' he said.

Rick and the others might have been having a great time, but now all I wanted was to get revenge for Danny. I had managed to convince a couple of girls I knew to give me a lift to Letchworth, and Rick, despite his best efforts to talk me out of it, decided to tag along. He was loyal; he wasn't a troublemaker, but if I was in trouble he was always right there, backing me up 100 per cent.

The girls dropped us off in town and we started the half-mile walk towards Martin's house. I hadn't planned this very well, as Rick repeatedly reminded me on the way. But I'd made up my mind. He knew as well as I did that I wasn't going to budge.

We arrived at Martin's family home around midnight and, with a balled fist, I gave the front door a hard bang. I kept banging until I had the attention of the whole house. Martin's dad wanted to know what it was about, and I made a feeble excuse about wanting to put something right and get the mess all cleared up. He made the mistake of opening the door. Within seconds, Rick and I were in his living room.

Martin came downstairs in his boxers, and I sat on the sofa with my half-empty bottle of beer. Rick, as always, positioned himself so he could cover whatever move I made. An argument immediately ensued, with me doing most of the shouting. Very quickly it became obvious that we weren't getting anywhere. I'd had enough of all the excuses – I lunged at Martin with my bottle, but he managed to take most of the swing in his shoulder rather than his head – which is what I had aimed for. He desperately pushed past Rick and legged it straight out of the front door, closely followed by Rick and me. But again, due to our drunken condition, he got away. We didn't hang around either, and thought it best to make a run for it before someone called the police.

We managed to get within a few hundred yards of my house when, sure enough, the police pulled us over and threw us in the back of the car. I knew I was stuffed. I had been out of jail for five days and now, while on licence, I had caused a scene at Martin's family home. We were taken to the police station, booked in, and told to sleep the booze off before being interviewed. As I lay down in my cell, I remember feeling gutted – I'd made such a bad job of the revenge attack, but I felt even worse that I'd involved poor Rick.

Rick was bailed, but it came as no surprise that I wasn't. I was held in Hitchin Police Station until the Monday for court. I decided this time, though, to plead not guilty and fight this one at trial. I reckoned I could intimidate Martin's family so they'd drop their accusations. I was right. After what I felt was a miraculous not guilty verdict at court, I again headed to the town to celebrate. I spent a few weeks on bail at my uncle's in south-east London. I still didn't think that Martin had been fully paid back, though.

## Bad Friday

A few months passed, and I began to settle into life on the outside again. I was working full-time once again for my dad's roofing company. I was still drinking most nights, but not as much as I had been before. However, rivalry and tension were brewing between the boys from the Jackmans and the Grange estates. It had been going on for years, but was getting worse. I knew it wouldn't be long before someone got badly hurt.

It was Good Friday, but ironically it ended up being a very bad Friday. Early in the day I met up with a couple of pals in a pub in  Baldock – Liam, who I'd been in prison with, and a lad called Matt. All the others were meeting in Letchworth, but because I had been put on a police-enforced ban of every pub in Letchworth town, due to the violence that followed me, Baldock was my only option. Baldock was by no means a stranger to this violence, but there were one or two pubs that would still let me in, if I wasn't with a big group.

We had a few pints and made our way to another pub. We'd only been in there a short while when a few of the other Jackmans boys stormed in, ranting about the fact that some of the Grange boys had just jumped them in another pub. This wasn't on, and we all started to plan our attack. I wanted to get a few car-loads of guys and some weapons, and steam into their local on the Grange estate, taking them by surprise – but they beat us to it.

I remember looking up from our table and there stood eight or nine Grange boys, about ten yards away. For a few moments you could have heard a pin drop. They certainly hadn't come for a pint. They'd come well prepared with lumps of wood, bottles, the lot. All we had was what was close at hand – tables, chairs and ashtrays.

The scene that followed made the front page of the local paper. They said it was like a Wild West show. There was blood everywhere. The bar staff ran for their lives, as did most of the customers. Those that stayed had no choice but to fight or get hurt – I pulled one lad's top over his head and punched him. Eventually we got on top of the Grange boys, and they started to leg it out of the door. It must have taken us a few minutes to get our heads together, and then we gave chase. I picked up a wooden bar stool as a weapon and we ran after them up the high street. What happened next I'll never forget, although I really wish I could.

They all ran towards the train station except one lad who thought he could escape by running up an alleyway. He obviously didn't know it was a dead end, but I did. I grabbed a few of the others and we went after this lad. He quickly realized his mistake and as he turned around to face us, the look on his face said it all. Cornered, impossibly outnumbered and face to face with his enemy, he could only lift his arms up in a gesture of surrender. We weren't in the mood for that, though.

I was the first to approach him. Armed with the bar stool, I coldly cracked him round the side of the head with it, knocking him out instantly. Then the others jumped in. He was repeatedly kicked in the head and face and had pint glass after pint glass smashed into his head from point-blank range. By the time we had finished with this lad, he wasn't moving at all, and had blood pouring out of his ears, nose and mouth.

I walked away from that scene convinced that he was dead and we were all going to jail for life. I am convinced it was only by the grace of God that he didn't die.

For such a serious crime it wasn't going to be long before the police hunted us all down and arrested us. And, sure enough, they did. I was the last to be charged, as I managed to avoid their raids on several occasions. But they were determined to get me for this one, especially after the not guilty verdict I had received a few months earlier. I recall one early-morning raid at my home when the police came in force. They stormed in and looked all over the house and garden for me, but failed to check the wardrobe I had been hiding in. I bragged about that for months.

Eventually, two close friends of my dad who were high up in the CID, arranged with him to meet me in a pub out in the countryside. So I turned up with my dad, full of arrogance and pride, to listen to what they had to say. They informed me that they were there unofficially and I was free to leave at any time, but they strongly advised me to go to the station with them, as it would go in my favour at court. I had always preferred to make my own favour at court, but Dad encouraged me to go with them and get it over with, so I reluctantly agreed.

When I arrived at the station, however, it was obvious I wasn't going anywhere in a hurry, and I was thrown in a cell for the weekend. I was very angry with the so-called 'friends' of my dad. I made sure I let them know that, but it didn't get me anywhere.

I was charged with GBH and violent disorder – this time I was facing a minimum of five years, which my barrister told me could end up being a lot longer. I was bailed to reappear and no one could believe it, least of all me. I had a terrible record for violence and should have been remanded in custody, but I certainly wasn't going to complain. I was out of jail for the moment and knew there was only one thing that could help me now – and that was to frighten and intimidate the witnesses. So one of my friends and I took the main witness out for some 'lunch'. By the time we had finished, he was fully agreeing that it was in everyone's best interest if he changed his statement at the last minute. The judge was furious and commented that it was obvious what had happened, but he knew there was nothing he could do about it. We all walked from court free men. We didn't leave, though, without a few choice words to the detectives in charge of the case. They responded threatening to get us all, soon.

# 5

# Grief

After that, life was fine for a while. I made a point of keeping my nose relatively clean, and I was working hard for my dad on the roofs.

It was 20 July 2000 and I had been working on a roof in Stevenage. It was a really hot day, and I knew my dad was under a lot of pressure to get the job done ASAP. He was in a bad mood, and I decided that I'd do all I could to get the job finished. It was a simple roof, really. A straight up-and-over with one chimney and four verges, but it had old Double Roman tiles on it and these things were not light. In fact, they were real back-breakers, but I wanted to help Dad out so I went for it, bombing the tiles straight off the roof into our open-backed lorry.

I was at it all day while Dad's two tilers were laying the new tiles on the other side. We used to have a real laugh at work, the three of us, and I got on really well with them, but today I was on a mission, so I got stuck in. You see, Dad had been unwell for some time. His heart was really bad and I'd been living in fear that he was going to die and leave me. I loved my dad so much; he was my hero. But on that particular Thursday afternoon he was being really sharp and nasty. He'd often be like that when he was under pressure at work or if he wasn't feeling well. Dad didn't know how to rest, so if he was having bad chest pains, he'd try to just shrug them off, pop a few painkillers in his mouth along with a sedative to calm him down, and carry on with whatever needed doing. But I could always tell. I could see the fear in his eyes that he was going to die. I'd become used to seeing fear in people's eyes, but this was different. He looked really scared – and that really scared me.

Dad told me to get into the lorry and go with him to empty it at a yard in Welwyn. I hopped in, pleased with myself and the work I had done that afternoon. I thought I would at least be congratulated, but the thanks never came. What came out of his mouth I won't repeat, but it wasn't nice. He was shouting and swearing at me all the way, and normally I would have shouted back, but this time I didn't. I was really scared that he was going to have a heart attack and I pleaded with him to calm down. For a minute he did, and then he pulled into a petrol station to fill up. He asked me which side the petrol cap was on and I looked out of my window. I was sure I could see it on my side, but after he positioned the lorry, he discovered it was the opposite side. After totally losing his temper, the last thing my dad said to me that day –

and indeed the last thing he ever said to me – was that I was a 'useless !*#*'.

The rest of the journey seemed to take forever. I ignored him all the way there and all the way home. I jumped out of the lorry as we pulled up at our house, and he drove off to price up some more jobs. It was to be the last time I saw my dad alive.

## Mrs Joy, I Have Some Bad News . . .

It was about 9.15 p.m. and Mum was moaning that Dad's dinner was getting ruined.

The knock at the door made me jump and, as I went to answer it, I had a quick look through the peep-hole first. I could make out two police officers – one was a uniformed WPC and the other was CID. Initially I thought they had come to check I was sticking to my curfew but then I realized that they had not . . .

They asked to speak to Mrs Joy and I showed them to the living room where my mum was sitting. I walked into the kitchen and knelt down on the floor. I went into a sort of trance, but my mum's screams soon brought me round. All I could hear her shrieking was, 'He wasn't saved! He wasn't saved!' It was years later before I understood what she meant.

I ran into the living room, after punching the door, and shouted at my mum to pull herself together. I was in shock and couldn't accept what the police were saying. My sister, Tracey, had collapsed on the floor and I was trying to pick her up. All the time I was telling them to get a grip and to stop crying. Crying was for wimps – or at least, that was what I had been taught by Dad.

I left the police to deal with my mum and sister and went out into the garden for some air. I decided to ring Rick and let him know – and my cousin David. They were both really close to my dad. I can't remember who I rang first. I just remember the tears coming once I had let my guard down. I was in bits. It started to hit me that I wasn't going to get the chance to make up with Dad.

The next day I had to go down to the local café where we all met before work and talk to the men. I hadn't had any sleep and I must have looked terrible, but a lot of them already knew and were devastated. My dad had a lot of faults but he touched many, many lives. I never really appreciated just how many until the day of the funeral.

I had been out the night before with Jamie, and he had stayed over at my house to support me. In the morning we got ready and greeted people as they turned up at the house. I had been to see Dad at the chapel of rest and was finding it hard to get the images of him lying dead in that box out of my head. I had written him a letter telling him how much I loved him and how sorry I was that I'd killed him – I was convinced that the stress I had caused him had given him the heart attack. I remember kissing his forehead and I can still remember how cold it was. But not as cold as my heart became after that.

## Goodbye Dad

By the time the hearse arrived, there were loads of people on our drive and lining up along the street next to the house. Leanne had come, and cheered me up momentarily by saying how good I looked in my suit but inside I felt as though I was dying. I was trying to be strong for my family but it was so hard.

The hearse drove slowly down to the church at the bottom of our road, and as I looked out of the window of the car that was carrying me and the immediate family, I felt really proud. Obviously I was upset, but I remember thinking how many people must have loved my dad. The traffic came virtually to a standstill as people were not only walking on the pavement alongside the hearse but also in the middle of the road in front of and behind the funeral cars. Many of my dad's friends were already waiting outside of the church, and by the time the service was due to start, the place was packed and people were crowding outside. Lots of my friends were there, not only to support me but also to pay their respects to my dad, who always got on really well with them.

The service was amazing. It was very emotional but touching as well, especially when a lady called Elaine who my mum knew from church got up and sang. She was a very talented singer and blew us all away with her version of 'Amazing Grace'. By the time she had finished there wasn't a dry eye in the church.

After the service we all made our way to the cemetery for the burial. It was only when they began lowering my dad into the ground that reality truly hit me. I could feel my heart going cold and I knew I would never be the same again.

After the funeral, everyone was invited back to the Three Horseshoes pub which was my dad's local in a little village called Willian. They had put on a lovely spread, but luckily we'd had the foresight to ask the pub opposite to provide food as well. Hundreds of people turned up. In fact there were so many that not only were both pubs full, including their gardens, but tons of people were milling around on the street outside. It was starting to get a bit overwhelming, so eventually I left with a few friends and went to another pub, where we steamed straight into a bag of cocaine and a load of booze.

The next few days became a blur as I hid from my feelings behind drink and drugs. In fact the next few weeks continued in the same way. I had hardened my heart to try and block my emotions out and the only place I felt safe was in the pub. I didn't realize it then, but my life was about to take an even more violent and sinister turn.

## Narrow Escape

As I look back on my life, I can see just how close I came to dying through the violence and the drugs. I remember the day I very nearly killed myself, as well as two of my best friends. I'd been out drinking all day with the boys and, as usual, had taken far too many drugs, when I started thinking about my dad and getting very emotional. Earlier in the day there'd been some trouble, so I'd already got tooled up, just in case. I had a gun in my waistband and a huge Rambo-style knife in my jacket. I was sitting at a table in a pub, armed like something out of the *A-Team*. My head was all over the place and I started to feel more and more frustrated. I knew I was worth more than this. Even though I was sitting there with some of my best mates, I felt sheer desperation and loneliness inside. I knew I was missing something. I tried brushing the feeling off by assuming it was just me missing my dad, and to a certain degree I'm sure it was, but there was something else that I needed. What was it? I shrugged off my thoughts as best I could.

Rick wanted to go home, so I said I'd give him a lift. I didn't have a car but that had never stopped any of us before. My mate threw me the keys to one of the cars which belonged to our friend Tony, and I drove off with Rick and another mate, Des, to Rick's house.

Suddenly, I decided that I wanted to visit my dad's grave, which was on the way. I pulled up and told the others to wait in the car. I left the gun and the knife in the car, as well as the wraps of coke and pills I had on me, stashing them all under the driver's seat. I didn't want to talk to my dad with that lot on me. That was far too disrespectful.

I walked up to the place where he was buried and knelt down beside it. I spent a few minutes crying on the headstone and asking him to forgive me for the way I was behaving. I promised, as I always did, that I'd pull myself together and turn my life around. Then I wiped my face with my sleeve, stood up and headed back towards the car. As I got back in the driver's seat I tried my best to hide my red eyes and set off towards Rick's.

We turned onto a long, straight country road with fields on either side. I remember putting my foot down and racing towards the other end. My eyes were fixed on the road but my mind was fixed on my dad. I vaguely recall hearing the others in the background screaming at me to slow down as we neared the junction at 90 mph. As I came out of the trance, it was way too late. I slammed on the brakes with both feet, but there was no way we were stopping. I shouted something like 'Hold on!' as we flew straight across the junction straight towards a solid wall on the other side. We hit it head-on.

Des, who was sitting in the back with no seatbelt on, was thrown violently forward, ending up in the front with me and Rick. It was a miracle he didn't go straight through the windscreen. Amazingly, we all crawled out of the car with hardly a scratch on us. Rick and I did suffer whiplash, but we were very lucky to be alive. The car was a write-off, and how the three of us weren't as well, I'll never know. We could see concerned people looking out of their bedroom windows at us, and as we all managed finally to regain our senses, we thought it best to make a run for it. After all, it wasn't my car. But I'd only run a few yards when I suddenly remembered the weapons and the drugs. I sprinted back to get them. I remember scurrying around, with my hands in the footwell of the badly damaged car, feeling for the stuff. First I found the coke, which went straight in my trouser pocket. Then came the gun, down under the waistband. But however hard I searched, I couldn't find the knife. Where was it?

I started to panic. At first I thought it might have been sent flying out of the car, but there was no way I was leaving it at the scene. I wasn't going to leave Tony to explain it – the poor bloke didn't have anything to do with it. I searched frantically for what seemed like a lifetime until finally, and with a sigh of relief, I found it. I used the sleeve of my jacket to quickly wipe any fingerprints from the door handles and the steering-wheel and ran off again. I caught up with Des, who was in a nearby field waiting for me. Rick had run the other way towards his house.

After a while, as we ran through the fields we could hear a helicopter in the distance, along with the sound of sirens. I wasn't willing to take the chance of being caught with what I had on me. I broke the gun down while wiping my fingerprints from it, and scattered it in the field. I chucked the knife away as well. I reluctantly did the same with the drugs, and we headed to the far end of the field where we could hide in the trees.

We scrambled up and hid there for a good half hour until we watched the helicopter fly away and heard the last siren disappear off into the distance. I phoned a mate to come and get us. I told him roughly where we were and he came speeding up not long after. Once in his car we were able to relax a bit, and we explained what had happened while he dropped us at our houses.

Walking through my front door, I tried to work out what I should do. I decided to phone the police to report my friend's car as stolen. I told them it had been on my driveway, as he had left it there that day so we could go out drinking, and when I got home it wasn't there. That way, I thought that if there were any prints still on it, they could be explained. After the call, I got undressed to go to bed. As I went to toss my jeans on the floor, I discovered a gram of cocaine still in my pocket, and rejoiced as I opened it and started to polish it off.

The next time I saw Tony's car was when we went to see it at the scrap yard. The man at the yard explained that if it hadn't been such a heavily built car whoever had been in it when it crashed would not have survived. I must admit it scared me a little when I saw the state it was in, but not enough for me to do anything about my lifestyle.

## Hooligans

September 2000 was the date, and Germany was the venue – Munich to be exact. The tension and expectation was really high: England v. Germany in the group stages of the European Championships.

I was a devout fan of Chelsea Football Club, and although I no longer went to their matches as regularly as I did when I was younger, I'd love nothing more than a trip to Stamford Bridge with my cousin, hoping for a good fight. I followed England, too. If ever my friends and I decided to go to an England game, we knew there was a good chance that there would be trouble. But that was part of the reason why we went. However, England v. Germany in Germany had a different smell to it altogether. There would be real rivalry, and we were all psyched-up for it. There were about ten of us. Due to the top-notch security it was a real mission for us to get into the country, but as we were all very determined, we soon found a way.

Upon arriving, we decided to dump our bags in the hotel and head straight out to hit the local bars. It wasn't long before we were all completely lashed and well on our way to finding some trouble. But nothing actually came of it that night.

The next day, I managed to find a shop well away from the area of the game and bought myself some CS gas. Gas was one of my favourite weapons, as it was quite possible to take out half a dozen blokes with a few squirts. I made sure I kept it safely tucked away ready for any action. We all got into some serious drinking, and I got into some serious drug abuse as well. I soon came to regret it, though, because by the time everyone was ready to go back to the hotel and get changed ready for a night out, I was in a bad way. It wasn't just that day – I'd been hard at it for a good week non-stop, and now it all finally caught up with me. I could hardly move from my bed as the others all left for some action. I was gutted but I knew I was in no state to do anything if it all kicked off, so I thought it best to rest and be ready for the next day. The rumour was that we'd all group up and fight some Germans.

However, it wasn't long before the lads came flying back into the hotel screaming blue murder about some gang from the Midlands or somewhere that had taken a liberty with one of our boys, and Tony had got stuck in to them. They wanted to regroup and go back tooled up. I was ill, but Tony wanted me on board with my gas, so I got up, threw on some clothes and armed myself with my can of 'squirt'. I really wasn't up for it one little bit, but I was caught up in this revenge attack and there wasn't a great deal I could do about it. Thankfully, there was no sign of this gang and we ended up going back to our rooms and swearing revenge for the next day.

The next day came and we all made our way to the pub where all the English were meeting up. From very early on, the place was packed with lads, all hell-bent on the same thing – drinking, abusing the locals, and eventually kicking off with the Germans or, better still, the local police. There was lots of booze and chanting. The atmosphere was getting more and more tense, and I could tell that it wouldn't be long before the fun started. I was right.

Out of nowhere, loads of riot police marched around the corner and stood opposite the pub we had taken over. Tony was on the ball, as usual, and managed to grab me and the others and get us outside seconds before the police stormed in the front entrance and unloaded a shower of tear gas.

Once we were outside, we grouped together with some other England supporters, about fifty or sixty strong, and all agreed that we should get stuck in to the police. We came face to face with them late afternoon. We had a ton of empty beer bottles we'd been collecting for such a time as this, and as both sides clashed, the police stood their ground and dropped their riot shields to absorb the scores of bottles we threw at them. They withstood the majority of our onslaught, but one or two were getting caught by the beer bottles raining down on them. Once we'd run out of ammo, they picked up their shields and charged us, emptying tons of gas in our direction. We had no choice but to run and take cover. Apart from the fact that I saw a few lads get their heads cracked open by some 'over the top' riot police officers, it was a relatively successful operation. We all had a few beers that night and waited for the game the following day.

On the morning of the game we were all buzzing with excitement. None of us had any tickets to get in, but we fancied our chances with the touts, and we weren't disappointed. We all paid about £100 each for our tickets and made our way to the ground. I still had my can of gas and made a pact with the lads that

I wouldn't enter the stadium until I'd squirted a German. I noticed a lad walking behind us and turned round to let him have it, but as he started screaming in pain, I realized he was actually English. I never was the brightest spark, but looking back, I can see just how crazy I was. I had an irrational hatred for Germans because of a war that took place many years before I was born and because of a game of football they beat us at.

The game was amazing. The tickets we had meant we were in the German end, and seeing as we beat them 5–1 it was a miracle we got out alive. Believe me, we didn't make a secret of the fact that we were English. We hurled abuse at them each time a goal was scored. After the match, there was very little trouble so we all made our way to the hotel, ready to leave for home.

Once we were back in England, I really started to hit the cocaine hard. I was still grieving over my dad and went into self-destruct mode. I was in the pub every night and my drug habit was becoming difficult to fund. I started to sell a few grams here and there to help me pay for my own supply, and this seemed to keep me going. But the more I took, the more I wanted, and after a few months it was obvious to everyone that I had a serious habit, although I always did my best to hide it.

By now I had the family home to myself. Mum had remarried quite quickly, and had left me, aged 22, in charge of the house, which was a big mistake. It was only a matter of weeks before I had rented out all the rooms to friends – the extra money helped fund my habit. But after a few months, I started to suffer awful side-effects from the drug abuse – often losing my temper for no reason.

My family were worried sick and were constantly praying for me, but I didn't want to know about God. After all, he was the one who had taken my dad away from me! I used to get really angry whenever the words 'God' or 'church' were mentioned, and shouted all sorts of abuse at my mum and my sisters (who had also become Christians). I was convinced they had all been brainwashed.

# 6

# Prison Again

The 2002 World Cup was now well under way and everyone was excited. Due to my now out-of-control habit, there was no way I could afford to go to Japan. I was offered a loan from one of the lads but I thought it best to stay put, so I ended up staying in Letchworth. I decided I could make loads of easy money selling drugs to everyone, and still enjoy the football by watching it in one of the pubs.

It was the night before England v. Argentina. I hadn't slept for two days. I had a gram of coke on me and I felt compelled to take it. By the time I was supposed to leave to meet my cousin at the pub, I was already in a mess. I had a quick wash and tried to make it look as if I hadn't been on a three-day binge. The last thing I needed was any trouble that day – I was on police bail again for another fight I'd had; one that resulted in me being charged with racially aggravated ABH and carrying an offensive weapon.

On that occasion I'd been watching Chelsea v. Liverpool, and Chelsea had been beaten 1–0. I'd ended up totally losing it and had thrown a glass behind the bar, smashing the optics bottles. Then I had walked outside, turned back around and smashed the pub window, sending glass all over some poor unsuspecting blokes on the pool table. I'd then gone home to get a tool because I wanted a row with someone. Anyone would have done. So, after arming myself with a chair leg, I'd walked into a local hotel and got myself a drink. Everyone could tell I was on a mission, and were staying out of my way. I could hear a guy talking in a foreign language to some blokes staying at the hotel, and this was all the excuse I had needed. It was bad enough that Chelsea had been beaten by the Scousers, but now a load of foreigners were in this bar! I'd shouted some abuse to get their attention and was told by a local to shut up, which was all I had needed to start a fight. The poor bloke didn't see my left hand coming, or the follow-up swing to his head with the chair leg. He had crashed to the ground, smashing into the glass doors. This was no small bloke, either. He was over six feet tall and heavily built, so he really hurt himself when he hit the floor. Two of my mates had grabbed me and we ran out of the bar. Within a few minutes we'd heard the ambulance approaching, followed by the police. Needless to say, I soon found myself arrested once again, and bailed to reappear at the magistrates' court in Stevenage.

So, since that incident, I had been trying to keep out of trouble. As I walked into the pub in Baldock, I promised myself that I'd behave. What happened next was not instigated by me. We found ourselves a nice table with a good view and settled down with some drinks to watch the match. Then, two women started shouting abuse at a girl on my table, and that annoyed me. Not the fact that they were shouting at the girl – but while it was going on, I couldn't see the football. I politely told them to shove off and leave her alone, which they did. To be honest I had completely forgotten about the whole thing after England went 1–0 up, and it took me by surprise when the door of the pub flew open and the son of one of the women marched towards me.

We both agreed it would be better to go outside and sort it out, rather than disturb everyone. When we got outside, the fun started. Loads of people got involved, and me and this lad were trying to get at each other. But eventually my cousin frogmarched me back into the pub and we carried on watching the match.

After the game, and a great win, the pub just seemed to erupt. People were dancing around hugging each other and going wild. But it wasn't long before I started to feel the last three days catching up with me. I needed to get home and sleep it off.

I made my way to the high street to find a taxi. As I approached another pub, the same lad came walking out with a couple of his mates and made a beeline for me. Now he was a tough lad, though it wouldn't have made much difference because of the state I was in. He hit me square in the face and we both started scrapping. Fortunately, his friends decided to break it up, which was good for me because I really wasn't getting anywhere. But it didn't stop me wanting to try. I knew I would need either back-up or a good weapon, so I decided the best idea was to go home and get a tool of some sort, then go back and finish the fight off.

I started the walk home, which was about a mile, but I saw a lad I knew driving past and flagged him down. He wasn't really a friend of mine, but he could see it was best to go along with what I wanted and he drove me to my house. I made him wait outside while I went in and got what I needed.

My sister, Nichola, and her husband were staying there, with my two nieces. They were all begging me to calm down, as they could plainly see I was raging. By this time the fight had pretty much sobered me up, and all I wanted was revenge. I went to my shed and looked around for a weapon. I was spoilt for choice, as I always made sure I had a good selection for such a time as this.

I'd recently borrowed a gun from a pal of mine for intimidation purposes. It was a real gun but it couldn't fire, which is probably the only thing that stopped me getting life that day. I shrugged off my nieces as they screamed at me to stay at home and leave it, and jumped back into the car. The look on the lad's face, when I got into his car with a Beretta hand gun, foaming at the mouth and ordered him to drive me back to Baldock, was a picture.

My head was pounding as I got out of the car and all I wanted to do was to teach the guy who had picked a fight with me a lesson and show everyone else that they shouldn't mess around with Rob Joy. I was on a massive ego trip. As I was pacing up and down Baldock High Street with the gun in my waistband, I started to realize that I could get into serious trouble for this, but I shrugged off the little sense I had, and marched towards the pub.

I had it all planned in my mind. I'd fly through the doors of the pub, make everyone get on the floor, and then smash this lad up. Thankfully it didn't happen that way. In fact he wasn't even in the pub, because he'd already been warned that I was looking for him. He came from the opposite direction and took me by surprise.

'What are you going to do, Joy? Shoot me?'

If the gun had worked, I think I would have put a bullet in him there and then. But I had to think fast, so I hit him on the side of the head with the butt of the pistol, cutting his head open. We wrestled to the floor and one of his mates managed to kick the gun out of my hand. I suddenly found myself in a dodgy situation. I was unarmed and outnumbered. I finally managed to get to my feet, after a clumsy wrestle, and got away. I ran to another pub and tried to get my head together.

There I was with a bloody face, a trainer missing and everyone staring at me in shock. I ran into the toilets to get cleaned up and phoned a pal of mine from Stevenage. He told me to stay put and he'd be straight there. So I laid low and waited until I saw him pull up in the car park.

The police had been driving up and down for a while now, and I knew I had to get away fast. I started to walk out of the pub, but didn't even make it to the car. Armed police came from everywhere, and within minutes I was handcuffed and in the back of a riot van. I couldn't believe it. I knew I was in big trouble this time. They had the gun, statements and even my trainer that had come off during the fight.

At the station I was told to make myself comfortable, as I wouldn't be going anywhere in a hurry. As I lay on the wooden bench in my cell, I realized that there was no way I was getting out of this one. I'd been caught red-handed, and even though the gun could no longer fire, it was still classed as a firearm, and this carried a minimum sentence of five years. On top of that were the charges made by the lad for the ABH that I was already on bail for. I had a horrible feeling that I wouldn't see the outside world again for a good few years.

I was put on remand at HMP Bedford and was under no illusion that I would get bail this time. My barrister was one of the best in the country, but he knew there was no point in even applying for it. On top of the racially aggravated ABH, I was now also charged with GBH and possession of a firearm. Things were not looking good.

However, luck, as it seemed at the time, was on my side. The CPS (Crown Prosecution Service) people were the same ones I'd had a couple of years previously, and they were worried I'd get to the witnesses again and walk free if it went to a trial. So they asked my barrister if I wanted to strike a deal. They said they'd drop the gun charge if I pleaded guilty to the ABH and GBH. I could still expect anything up to seven years, but at least now my barrister could work his magic and I had a chance of a smaller sentence. I was given a sentencing date and waited on D Wing of Bedford Prison until I had to appear at court. Bedford Prison was a dump, but I knew a few people in there and, as it was my local jail, it was convenient for visits.

It wasn't long before I was due for sentencing. When the day arrived, I got ready and was taken to Luton Crown Court. I was nervous by now, as I had been told which judge it was – he knew me, and he could be really hard on people he didn't like. In these situations I knew it was always best to expect the worst, so I geared myself up for a five-year stretch. However, at the last minute I was told that this judge was ill and another one had been called in. The sentence was read out. Twelve months for the racially aggravated ABH and twelve months for the GBH, to run consecutively. Two years in all. Only two years! I was buzzing. I looked over at my friends and family, and although they all looked gutted, I couldn't help but smile. Yeah! I might have two years ahead of me, but I'd only serve half and there was a new tagging system which meant if I kept my nose clean, I could be out in less than a year.

The 'sweatbox' (prison security van) took me back to Bedford and reprocessed me as a convicted prisoner. Bedford is a 'local' prison, which means many of its inmates are there on remand or waiting to be relocated, so it was only a couple of months before I was told to pack my bags and move to HMP Wayland in Norfolk. This place had a great reputation. It was a Category C working prison, and everyone I spoke to who had been there said it was a good prison.

After spending about three weeks on the induction wing, I was moved to the main wing and put in a single cell on the ground floor. Within a day or two, I had cleaned the cell up nicely, and had a few of my photos and a couple of posters to brighten the place up a bit. This was very different to my first experience of prison. Being an adult jail, it was a lot calmer. Most of the guys just wanted to settle down and get their time served without any trouble, although there was the odd bully boy and Jack the Lad.

## HMP Wayland

I had a different attitude to jail this time round. I just wanted to get my sentence out of the way ASAP. I had a few months to get myself off the drugs. Once I was out, I had plans to set up a legal business, start a family and basically turn my life around. I started to dream of owning my own gym, running a nice little business and making my life worth living.

At the time I still had a passion for weight training. Wayland had a really good gym, so I decided to join and really go for it.

I had a few scams going on my wing, which meant I had a lot more money to spend each week on my canteen sheet. I'd order tins and tins of tuna, cans of nourishment drinks, and packets of noodles. I'd learnt that there was no point in training unless you were going to fuel your body with the right food, so I became obsessed with eating. I had a job on the servery, serving food at meal times, which meant that when there were tons of leftovers, I could take them back to my cell. I used to have £10 a week sent in to a lad on my wing who worked in the kitchens and he'd supply me with twenty eggs a day. He'd sneak them back and hide them in my cell for when I finished work. He also got me extra bananas and tuna now and then, and I'd make myself protein shakes using ten raw eggs, a banana and a can of nourishment drink. I'd shake it up in a bottle and guzzle it down. I'd eat tuna and noodles twice a day, too, and all the food I could lay my hands on at the servery. Sometimes I'd be so full I'd have to force the food down using a pint of water, nearly making myself sick in the process. But it was working as I was bigger than I'd ever been before, and my strength was really improving.

I was training six days a week with a guy called Scouse (who you can probably guess wasn't from London!). This guy was about 5 ft 5 in but really stocky. He was inside for kidnapping and torturing a gangster over the murder of one of his pals. But he was good to me. (He even sent me a new suit just after I got out of jail, to wear to my grandad's funeral. My grandad had died two days before I was released, and Scouse knew I wouldn't have time to buy one.) Scouse and I became really close, due mainly to our shared love of the gym, and he taught me how to bulk-up quickly. He really pushed me at every session. We spent a lot of time together during 'association' in another guy's cell, who was just as crazy as Scouse was. The three of us would plan ways of earning money, and I'd listen to their stories of selling drugs. They were both big-time dealers on the outside, and wanted me to work for them when I was released.

I wanted to get *really* big but, although I was eating like a horse, I wasn't able to get the protein that my body needed to develop at that kind of rate, so I asked around and found someone who could get me some steroids. A lad from another wing that I met at the gym said he had some from his last jail, which I could buy, so I arranged for the money to be sent to his mum outside. When she confirmed that the money had arrived, he handed over thirty tablets that he said were steroids. I was unsure of the quality of the tablets and very suspicious, as they had no stamp on them, but in my desperate hunger to increase my size,

I took them regardless and left him with a warning that if they weren't good, I'd be back to see him.

After a couple of weeks of seeing no noticeable difference, I was certain that I'd been ripped off. I showed the tablets to Scouse who agreed that this lad had conned me. Now I had only parted with £30, but it was the principle more than anything. I told the others that I'd sort it out during exercise, when I knew this guy would be out in the yard. I didn't need a great deal of psyching up, but Scouse and the others still did a good job anyway. I knew my reputation was at stake. In jail it's one thing keeping your nose clean, but if someone blatantly rips you off and you don't do anything about it, then everyone will start to try it on. No, I had to do something about this one.

Me, Scouse and a bloke called Baz went out to the yard and had a look round for this lad. It wasn't long before I spotted him walking on his own. It was now or never – the perfect opportunity for me to give this guy a slap, while he was all alone and well away from any screws. By the time I caught up with him, he only had enough time to flinch as I smashed a left hook into his chin, sending him flying. He managed to get back on his feet just as we were about to kick him to bits, and he ran towards the officers. The officers shouted to us all to get back to our wings. I went back to my cell and was patted on the back by the boys and reassured that they were right behind me if anything else came of it. I just wanted it to all be over, as I was only a month away from getting a decision on a tag. A tag meant that I could get out three months early. I was really hoping that I'd be accepted for a tag as up till now I'd stayed out of trouble. OK, I'd been put on report a couple of times for dodgy phone cards, but nothing serious, and the chances were I would be accepted – unless, of course, the guy I had just smacked grassed me up. He wasn't the sort, though, and after a while I was confident that the incident had been swept under the carpet and I could finish the rest of my sentence in peace.

## Making Plans

My mum had been flat hunting for me while I was in prison, with money that my dad had left me. She found a nice one-bedroom flat on the Jackmans Estate and sent the details in to me to see if I wanted to buy it or not. I agreed and she went ahead and finalized the purchase, which further increased my chances of getting the tag, as now I could say I had my own place. The tag meant I'd have to be home every night by 7 p.m. sharp, but that would be better than being stuck in jail full time.

However, I was mistaken about the incident with the fake steroid dealer being over. Apparently he knew some big lads on his wing and they wanted to get me back for what I had done to their mate. A warning was sent that they were planning to jump me when they next saw me, so I went to Scouse and Baz and let them know what was going on. They both seemed really excited about the possibility of a mass riot, and pulled me into the cell to discuss it. They started pulling out weapons that they had made and hidden in their cells. These guys were lunatics. They had moulded razor blades into the end of their tooth-brushes and had big lumps of wood. They even had toilet brushes sharpened to a point. You name it, they had it, and they were more than up for using them. I could see that this was going to get right out of hand, and I didn't want to lose face by telling them I just wanted to forget the whole thing. Don't get me wrong, at the time I didn't mind the odd fight – I just didn't want to lose the tag.

My girlfriend was beginning to feel the strain of constant visits and letter-writing, too. I had as good as promised her that I would be out in March rather than July. I had laid it on thick whenever she visited about how I had learnt my lesson this time and how, when I got out, we could settle down and start a family – and I meant it. I'd had enough of this life and just wanted to put it all behind me and raise a family. But now it looked as if I was going to have to risk it all for the sake of a measly £30.

The time was set for later that day. There were a few of them and a few of us and it was going to be settled once and for all. I tried my best to put it out of my mind and concentrate on the gym course I was doing. I'd passed a few grades already, and I was on my way to becoming a qualified weightlifting coach and fitness instructor. I received my certificate at the end of the session and managed to quickly do some weights before taking a shower and heading back towards Y Wing, ready for the fight.

In jail, though, it never turns out how you plan it. I walked into the toilet before I left the gym hall and was immediately followed in by the lad I had smacked and two of his mates. I was on my own, and unarmed. I knew I couldn't let them see I was worried, but there were three of them and they were all big lads. I feared the worst. By some miracle, though, I managed to argue my way out of the toilets without so much as a punch being thrown. It turned out that the lad didn't want any trouble either, and he was also just going along with it due to pressure from his wing. We decided to end it there, and the whole thing blew over.

## Grandad

Within a few weeks of the incident, I was called into the governor's office, and sat in front of him and my personal officer, in regards to my tagging application. They made me sweat for ages with reminders of the times I had been put on report and been abusive to staff and so on, but eventually I was told that as I had a flat ready to move into and a job offer which needed me to start as soon as possible, I had been accepted for early release and told I only had to serve another three

*Internal Revolution*

weeks. I was absolutely buzzing and was straight on the phone to my family to tell them the good news. I never did tell them just how close I was to losing the tag before I had it.

I was called into the office by my PO (principal officer) and told to sit down. It turned out my grandad was in hospital and didn't have long to live. He'd been asking for me and wanted to see me before he died. I had been really close to my grandad, and the news hit me hard. My PO promised he would put a good word in for me to the governor and see if they could get me out on day release. I was told it should-n't be a problem, as I was hardly a risk, as I was due out in about a week anyway.

I went back to my cell and grabbed my phone card so I could ring my mum. She confirmed that it didn't look good and all Grandad wanted was to see me one more time before he died. The news obviously upset me and I told my mum to tell him to hold on and I'd be there as soon as I could.

Then my PO came back to me and said the governor wasn't there and would return in the morning, but he practically guaranteed that I'd be allowed to go and see Grandad, come back, finish my last week and then be out officially. But the next day I was told that the gover-nor had heard all about it and refused me a day release, as he felt it was too risky and that I'd try to escape.

What! With only one week left of my sentence? I totally lost it and told the two officers in my cell to leave before I tore into them. They didn't argue, partly because they knew I was upset for good reason, but more because at that point, after having purchased some real steroids, I was looking like a pit bull. I had no neck and the veins in my body were pumped out due to the effects of the steroids. My temper was a lot harder to control, too. I'd always had a quick temper but with the strongest anabolic steroids you could take inside me, I was like a walking time bomb.

I swore to the officers that if my grandad died before I got a chance to see him, I'd do the lot of them. I was absolutely raging and, when my cell door banged shut, I let all my frustration out and wept. I'd reacted this way for years. I'd bottle it all up, then suddenly explode, or if I had no one to explode on, I would punch a wall or head-butt a pint glass or something. Anything to release the anger I had inside me. The amount of times I'd been taken to hospital after smashing pint glasses into my own forehead was ridiculous, and I'd broken many of the bones in my hands after attacking defenceless brick walls.

My grandad did die, two days before I was due out. I was in shock. His last wish had been to see me before he died and, due to the mess I had made of my life, I'd let him down. For the last few days of my sentence, I was bombarded constantly with thoughts of carrying out my threats against the officers. I had to gather every last ounce of sense and strength left in me not to fly into the governor's office and rip him apart. My mum calmed me down over the phone and pointed out that I'd feel even worse if I didn't go the funeral, just because I'd done some officers in. Mum made me laugh, because although she had been a Christian for about fifteen years now, she still talked just like me – without the swearing of course.

I managed to get released without any bother and met my sister Tracey outside the large iron gates. It was so good to see her. She'd gone to a lot of effort – even though it was the middle of March, there in the car were two big bags full of Christmas presents, still wrapped. She'd saved them for me, and I spent the whole of the journey back to Letchworth opening them. There were clothes, smellies, gadgets – all sorts. She really cheered me up and I started to have a natural high. Maybe this time I could stay away from the drugs and the mindless violence and make a name for myself, like my dad did after he gave up alcohol. By the time I arrived at the flat, I was really excited. I looked around my new home and started to truly believe I could actually do it. *This time* I could do it!

Who was I kidding?

My prison sentence, having money sent in to me while I was inside, and buying a flat, as well as paying off lots of debts, had put a huge dent in my inheritance. But it was nothing compared to the £250,000 I was about to blow up my nose, as my habit really started to take over.

# 7

# Paranoid

As I have already mentioned, towards the end of my sentence, I'd started taking steroids and was considerably bigger than when I went in. I'd developed a real passion for training and even had a dream of buying my own gym with the rest of the money from my inheritance. But that very quickly evaporated.

For the first three months of my release I was on tag, which, believe it or not, actually seemed worse than being inside. It enabled you to go to work and be free during the day, but you became a prisoner again after 7 p.m. After a couple of weeks, I started to hate it. All the lads met up early at the weekend and I'd join them, but just as things started to get lively I had to be indoors. It took one or two of my more sensible friends to convince me to go home after I'd had a few beers.

Apart from that, though, things were actually looking quite good for a while. I had a job as a hod-carrier on a new building site in Baldock, earning good money. My girlfriend and I were getting on well living together in the new flat and I was training really hard at the gym. I'd bought myself some more juice (steroids), and started to look like the Incredible Hulk's little brother. It was then that I started to get greedy.

## Debt Collector

A friend of mine was selling a fair bit of cocaine and asked me if I wanted to start collecting money for him. He gave me a list of names and the amounts that were owed, and I went to work collecting it all. After less than a week, I'd managed to collect around three-quarters of his money, and I hadn't even had to smack anyone. I just rang them up and told them who I was, that the debt had been passed over to me, and would they kindly get it to me straight away? It usually worked, but there was one lad who was beginning to drive me mad. He owed a lot of money and, quite frankly, I was getting fed up with all his excuses. Besides, until I got his money I wasn't getting paid, and I needed some cash to buy more drugs for myself. I'd started taking them again, after managing to go without for about four weeks. However, when I put myself in a place where drugs were all around me, it wasn't going to be long before I had a line up my nose.

I arranged for the guy whose debts I was collecting to pick me up early from work. I wanted to catch this lad as he came out of his workplace and surprise him. We waited for about half an hour, and were just about to give up when he came out. The second he saw us, he ran for his life. He sprinted across a field and we couldn't follow because we were in a van, but we decided to drive on and cut him off nearer his house. By the time we pulled up alongside him he was so out of breath that I had no trouble flinging him in the back of the van.

It was only a fifteen-minute drive to some woods I knew of, and I spent the time explaining exactly what I had in mind to do to him when we got there. There were loads of work tools in the back of the van and I was asking him to pick which one he wanted me to use on him. I also explained that I would leave him there, dead. It was all just a scare tactic, but I took pride in seeing how much I could frighten him as we drove to the isolated woods. When we arrived, I got out, dragged him out of the back, and threw him up against the van. I told him that this time he was allowed to live, but if the money wasn't there within seven days I would tie him to a tree and set him on fire.

The steroids, mixed in with all the cocaine I was consuming, were having a really negative effect on me. I was more violent and psychotic than I had ever been before. The worst thing was that I was really starting to enjoy it. I got a kick out of this way of life, and seeing fear in people's eyes excited me.

When the seven days were up and there was still no sign of the money I got on the phone and started chasing him up. Eventually he answered and said he'd be at my mate's flat in an hour. I prepared myself a 'Rob Joy Special' (that's what the lads used to call my lines of coke because they were so big) and waited for him to arrive. All I was supposed to do was take the money from him and hand it to my mate, but I had other plans in mind. I hadn't even told my friend what I intended to do.

When the guy eventually arrived, he passed me the money. I took it from him calmly with my left hand and then suddenly, with my right hand, slapped him clean round the side of his face. I wanted to humiliate him and get a warning out to any would-be bad payers. He fell onto the bed next to my mate and I dived straight on top of him, pulling a flick knife. I held it to his face and put my face right up against his, screaming at him whilst psyching myself up to actually cut his face open. But something deep inside me knew I shouldn't. Eventually I pulled the knife away and let him get up. He ran out of the flat, shaken up but relatively unharmed, and I stood up, trying to get my breath back. I was shaking with adrenalin. I'd never thought of using a knife before and I had scared myself. I'd hit people with lumps of wood, butts of guns and various other weapons. I'd even sunk my teeth into some guy's face before, but to me there was something much more sinister about sticking a knife in someone.

# Losing My Grip

After word got around that I was collecting for my mate, he rarely had bad payers. Soon after, though, he informed me that my services weren't required any more. Because of my own habit, however, I ended up owing a large sum to the same guy whose money I'd been collecting. My behaviour was getting more and more erratic, and everyone was starting to ask questions. Normally a drop in my size would have been a dead giveaway for my drug abuse, but because of the steroids I was taking, I managed to keep my weight stable, so it was longer before alarm bells started ringing in people's ears. Soon I'd lost another good job, due to missing days with 'comedowns' from the drugs. I had loads and loads of colds in as little as three months – actually, they were more like flu.

By now I'd had my tag removed and I was free to stay out and do whatever I liked. I got to a stage in my drug abuse where my grip on reality – of what I was doing and of life itself –  disappeared. I'd go for days without caring about the way I was treating anyone. It was only when I'd sniffed my last line in that particular session that the guilt started kicking in. I'd lie there for hours consumed with guilt about the way I'd been behaving and the people I was hurting but, without fail, the very next day I had forgotten all about it and the cycle started all over again. Welcome to the disgusting and seedy world of drug addiction.

At times I remembered my dad and wondered what he would think if he was looking down on me. I used to write stacks of poems about him when I was coming down from the coke.

> Thursday 20th of July 9 p.m. just gone,
> My heart told me something was wrong,
> My dad was late, his dinner cold,
> I watched my mum as we were told,
> Mrs Joy your husband's dead,
> Those words will never leave my head,
> I lost that day not just my dad,
> But the hero and best friend I had.

That was one of many I wrote as I looked back on my empty life. I longed for a way out of the mess I had created. The life I was living was completely destroying not only my body but my mind, too, as the deadly mixture of cocaine and steroids began to have a long-term effect on me. I started slipping deeper and deeper into the dangerous and crazy world of drug psychosis. I'd started to do far too much cocaine and my head just wasn't right.

## Supply and Demand

I met a guy who was a big dealer in the area, and because I was given a good 'reference'. I was able to get nine thousand pounds-worth of the highest quality cocaine, on credit. It was too good an opportunity to turn down, and I went into the deal with a friend who was keen to earn loads of money. For him, it was about the cash, but for me it was more about having the drug itself.

The day we were due to pick the gear up, I was really excited. I got a buzz out of making deals such as this. It made me feel like the gangster that in my childish mind I wanted to be. I'd watched far too many films where gangsters were glorified and made to look special. I took the phone call from this guy, and my friend and I drove off to meet him. We were told to meet at a quiet spot near town, where I would jump in his car while my friend followed. I was his contact, so he didn't trust my friend yet.

As we started to drive, I was given the lowdown. He had a bunch of conditions and regulations about how he wanted his business to operate. I was never to talk to him over the phone or mention real names when I spoke to anyone else. He was shifting kilos of this stuff and was probably being watched by every policeman for miles around. Eventually he handed over the bag stuffed with cocaine and promptly told me to get out of the car. I jumped straight into my friend's car and we headed back towards his house, where we could check out the gear properly. I could hardly contain myself as I started to unwrap this solid lump of top-class powder. It felt like Christmas-time. I lifted it up to the light and watched how it glistened and sparkled. It had all the right markings of the rocket fuel I had been promised.

The plan was to break it up and divide it into single grams, and then sell it on for £50 per gram. By our calculations that would make us an easy £3,600 profit. This was never going to be the outcome in practice, though – not with my habit! By the end of the week, and the day that the money was owed, we only had just enough to pay him. OK, we were owed a few quid here and there, perhaps £1,000 or so, but our figures were way off. My friend also liked the odd line, but nothing like the kind of quantity I used. We'd worked out that most of what we were owed belonged to him because the rest had gone up my greedy nose. But I was fine with that because I'd been wasted all week on the finest 'sniff'.

After a brief discussion we both sat down together and discussed ways to prevent me using so much next time and agreed to put safety measures in place to ensure we set the business up right. We decided to employ a couple of young lads to be runners for us. We knew, however, that doing that would seriously eat into our profits and we weren't particularly keen. So we came up with the idea of cutting the cocaine up and mixing it with something else to make it go further. However, I knew that the people I sold it to expected good quality stuff.

We went back and got a new lump of cocaine, paid for the previous one, and started again. This time we cut the lump in half. We kept one half pure for my customers, and the other half we cut with ground-up hay fever tablets. That way our profit would be the same, even after paying two lads to drive the stuff around. And it worked. I'd sit in my flat watching telly and sniffing huge lines, and every time the phone rang I'd arrange for one of my lads to drop the order to them. I'd make sure that I kept at least three generous grams for myself every night before I handed the rest over to my runners and set them up for the night's work.

Weekdays were reasonably busy, but come the weekend it went crazy. All the while, though, I was either at the flat or at a friend's, shovelling bucket-loads of the stuff up my nose.

Within three or four weeks things were getting out of hand. I was losing my grip big time, and started to become dangerously paranoid. I'd grill the two runners every time they came round to drop the money off and reload. I was convinced that they were ripping me off because the money never added up, no matter how hard we tried to work it out. It should have been simple. I gave them ten grams at a time to sell at £50 per gram and expected £40 per gram back, allowing them to keep £10 from each gram for themselves. When they sold out they were supposed to ring me and then meet me with the money. But they'd come round with £300 and swear that the other two grams had been given back to me. I, apparently, had phoned one of them after my three grams for personal use had run out and ordered two more for myself. This was getting ridiculous: I was polishing off five grams a night; I was going days without food, sleep or even a wash; I was now a full-blown junkie.

We were struggling to pay my supplier on time, but kept trying to buy more time with excuses of bad debts and people not paying. For every lump I got, I planned for it to make up for the last one. I was playing catch-up all the time and it was never going to work. Eventually my partner came to me and said he wanted out.

I decided to go it alone. I foolishly believed that I could take all the debt on and get myself out of the mess I was in. I changed my mode of operation slightly from that point, to try to limit the amount I could take myself. I got another close friend, who was the only one I felt I could trust at the time, to hold the cocaine for me. I had someone else holding the money for me and I took on another two lads for the drop-offs. But things started to go drastically wrong. The paranoia began to overtake me and I became convinced that I was being watched.

It seemed as if everywhere I went I was being followed and everyone around me was out to get me. I would lie in bed with a weapon in each hand, convinced that at any minute I was either going to be raided by the police or robbed by some other dealers. I was constantly gripped by fear: I was no longer the confident and bold man I used to be; I'd become scared of my own shadow; I was constantly running to the window checking for police helicopters and would-be assassins. I had completely lost the plot.

## Drug-Induced Madness

My sister, Nichola, convinced me to go with her to see a psychologist and tell him everything. After much persuasion, I finally agreed and walked into the bloke's office a quivering nervous wreck. He took one look at me and knew instantly that I was on drugs. My sister explained that I sometimes rang her at three in the morning, having a panic attack and trying to whisper to her that there were men in the flat trying to kill me. She began to cry as she spoke to him, and I remember realizing for the first time how my life was affecting my family. I was desperate for help, and desperate to kick my habit. The psychologist diagnosed me as developing paranoid schizophrenia and warned me that if I carried on the way I was, I would need to take anti-psychotic drugs for the rest of my life.

I was sent away with a prescription for tablets which, according to the packet, were for people who heard, saw or imagined things that weren't real. However, despite the fear that I could end up spending years locked away in a mental institution, I was powerless to quit the drugs. I sometimes managed to keep a lid on my habit for a few days at a time, but only because I was taking so many tablets. But I always ended up losing my resolve.

One night I came close to killing two of my best friends in a moment of madness. We'd been out drinking and I ended up back at my mate's house. Three of us were in his living room popping Ecstasy and sniffing loads of cocaine, when I started to lose it. Suddenly, and right out of the blue, I became paranoid that my two mates were planning to attack me.

Not only that, but I thought that they had arranged for other people to come round and kill me. They'd started talking quietly to each other – that's all – but my drug-crazed mind jumped to its own conclusions. I could see shadows of people sneaking up from the back of the house, through the curtains, and I ran into the kitchen and grabbed a huge knife from one of the drawers. I also armed myself with a police-style flick-kosh that was lying around, and sat down on the sofa next to one of them. They were trying not to provoke me, by avoiding looking directly at me or making any sudden movements that might make me flip. But it just made things worse, as I thought they were ignoring me.

I had the knife firmly gripped in my right hand, resting on the top of the sofa a few inches away from my mate's head, whilst all the time toying with the idea of sticking it straight in his face.

After a while I jumped up and ran into the kitchen, positioning myself so that I could see if anyone came in through either door. I waited there like a raging animal ready to pounce. Soon, one of my mates wanted to go to the toilet but I wouldn't let him, as I was convinced he was going to let people in through the window. At that point I knew I was in a bad way and I could feel a panic attack coming on. I tried in vain to calm myself down and pull myself together, but it seemed that this time I was too far gone.

Then, just as suddenly as it had come on me, it went – just like that – and I snapped out of it. My mates calmly explained to me that it was all in my head and that they were my friends. I dropped the weapons and burst into tears. My mate comforted me and held me until I my breathing was back to normal. He then put me to bed and sat with me until I'd fallen asleep.

When I woke up, we had a long chat about what had happened and he told me frankly that unless I gave up the drugs I was going to end up in jail for killing someone.

# 8

# God . . . and the Devil

I was spending a lot of time at my sister Nichola's house by this point, as she was trying to help me get sorted out. She took every opportunity she had to mention God and what he could do for me if I'd let him. I'd respond by asking her why God had let me get my life in such a mess and why, if he was real and if he loved me as much as she said he did, he hadn't done something about it and helped me get out of it. She explained that we all have our own free will and God never takes that away from us. She said that he desperately wanted to help me, but I had to invite him to do so. She explained that what she had wasn't a religion, it was a relationship with Jesus, and that she spoke to him and he spoke back to her. The idea freaked me out, and I thought she was more crazy than I was. Then, one day, just as she got to the top of the stairs, I remember her looking at me and saying that if I wanted to know if God was real or not, I should ask him – ask him for a sign to show me he was real.

I didn't have a clue what to ask for, so I went into her spare bedroom and put on a DVD. It was there in that little room that I had my first encounter with God. I asked him to give me a sign to prove to me that he was real and, sure enough, it came. Within a few minutes I remember feeling strange and suddenly found that I couldn't stop moving. I was not in control of my body at all. I stood up, sat down, rolled around on the floor, but was unable to stop what was going on. I tried several times to stop myself but I couldn't. It wasn't just what was happening externally either – it was the feeling I had whilst it was happening. Words can't really explain it, but at the time I just knew. I knew from that day on that not only was God real, but that he was fully in control – if I allowed him to be.

Now I had to decide what I was going to do about it. I told my sister what had happened and she arranged for two guys she knew to come and pray for me. It all seemed a bit sudden and weird – but what did I have to lose? The next day came and Mike and Pete turned up to pray for me. I felt like a right fool sitting there while these two guys were talking to me about Jesus. Mike explained to me very seriously that as Christians they had the authority to cast out all the demons that were in me, but if I went back to my old life it would be worse for me than it was before. He used scriptures from the Bible to explain it all properly. I was open enough to allow them to pray for me, but I refused point-blank to become a Christian.

So they prayed. Man, I didn't know what was going on! I thought praying was when you got down on your knees and politely asked God to do something for you. These two were in a different class! They commanded the devil to release me and asked God to set me free. They were like a couple of Christian ninjas.

Afterwards I realized that I needed to make a decision, either to carry on as before or to follow God. But thought to myself, *Well, I do believe in God now, that's enough isn't it? It doesn't mean that I have to go to church. All I have to do is be good.*

## All I Have to Do is Be Good

After that I was determined, really determined, to get clean and get my life back. I cut down drastically on the drugs and carried on taking the anti-psychotics. I even got myself a job on a new building site and started to put a bit of weight back on. My confidence came back as well and, after a couple of weeks, I decided to venture out for a drug-free night in Baldock, so I went to a hotel and had a few pints.

During the evening I found out that a friend of mine had been jumped by some Asian lads the night before, and I was not best pleased. There were some Asians sitting nearby, next to a pool table. I approached them and asked what they knew about the lad who was jumped the previous night. They swore it was nothing to do with them. I left them with a few threats as to what I'd do if I found out they were lying.

That was it, I thought – I was back! I felt really proud of myself. I convinced myself that I must be OK now I had God on my side and I accepted a line of cocaine from a friend. I ended up at a flat belonging to a girl I knew, where there was a bit of a party going on.

It was later on that night that I first spotted Rachel. She was sitting on the floor quietly, keeping herself to herself, not really talking to anyone. I was instantly attracted to her and wanted to find out more about her – I was no longer with Leanne; by this time we'd drifted apart – so I called Rachel into another room. We spent the next few hours talking and seemed to hit it off really well. By the morning I was totally convinced that she was the right girl for me. We swapped numbers and arranged to meet up the next day. Excited, I ironed my good shirt and made my way to meet her at her friend's house, but not before buying myself a quick half-gram. When I got there, she looked even lovelier than when I first set eyes on her, and I remember feeling certain that Rachel was going to be 'the one'. We spent the night drinking with her friend and her partner, and I ended up staying the night.

The next few weeks were amazing. I had really fallen for Rachel and we spent every minute we could with each other. It wasn't long before I was having dinner at her family home and we started getting more serious about each other. I was still doing the drugs, but nowhere near as much as I had before, and I was starting to enjoy life again.

During this time, though, I had to sell my flat. As a result of my habit I owed a lot of money and there was a threat out against me. I finally managed to pay all my debts off and ended up sleeping on a friend's sofa for the next few weeks. But that also meant I was left with some extra cash to burn – and I couldn't help but blow some of it. I went out and bought loads of new clothes and started to feel really good about myself.

## Close Call

Things were going great – that is, until I went out to Monaco to watch Chelsea play in the Champions League. Rachel was quite happy about me going, and I booked my flight along with my cousin David and some friends. I was really looking forward to the trip away and thought that I could make it a bit more interesting by smuggling a few grams of cocaine out there with me for personal use. After all, it was a special occasion.

The night before, I'd had a fair amount to drink as well as some 'sniff' and, as we had an early morning flight, I thought I would just go without sleep that night and sleep on the plane. We got to Luton Airport at about 6 a.m. and the bar was open, so we decided to get straight to work on the booze. All I was doing was topping up from the night before, so I was feeling quite drunk before we even got on the plane.

Once we were airborne the drink really started to flow and we got some champagne to toast the journey. Needless to say, I didn't get any sleep but by the time we arrived at the airport I felt fine. I'd already pushed myself way past the barrier, so to speak, and was now running on pure adrenaline.

We had the option of an hour's ride by taxi or bus to our hotel or a ten-minute helicopter flight straight from the airport to within half a mile of where we were staying. We all agreed on the helicopter and arrived in style. As soon as we'd dumped our bags in the rooms we went to find a bar, but not until I had retrieved my stash of drugs from inside my shampoo bottle. A 'Rob Joy Special' went up my nose, and I floated out of the hotel following the others to really 'start the session'. We never took it easy on trips like this, and it wasn't long before every one of us was absolutely steaming. I was helped along by a few lines of Peruvian Flake (top-class cocaine) and didn't seem to be feeling any effects from the large quantity of booze I was consuming.

My cousin and one of the lads made their way back to the hotel to get some sleep, so that they could be on good form for the football the next day, but the rest of us carried on into the early hours. At about 2 a.m., my two mates were sitting at our table and I was standing next to them when, all of a sudden, I started to feel really paranoid. There was a terrible pain in my throat, which made it hard to breathe; I began to feel really unwell. I rushed to the toilet and took a look at myself in the mirror. I was as white as a sheet and my eyes were all over the place. I turned towards the sink and started to bring up blood. It was so severe that I was fighting for breath. One of the lads came into the toilets to find me in a terrible state, and I hazily tried to explain what was going on whilst still gasping for breath. As the vomiting subsided, he quickly grabbed me by the arm, rushed me outside and held my head so he could have a look down my throat to check for blockages. There seemed to be a huge lump in the back of my throat that was almost entirely blocking my windpipe. The expression on his face told me that I was in trouble. He ran back to get our other mate and they tried to get me a taxi to the hospital. By this point I was terrified. I tried to tell them in-between the gagging that I couldn't breathe and they had to hurry. Rod literally jumped in front of a taxi and made the driver take us to the hospital.

In the back of that taxi I started to feel a lot calmer. My breathing was getting worse but I felt strangely peaceful. One of my mates tried to dislodge the lump in my throat by sticking his fingers down, but it didn't help at all. The lump was actually a swelling, not simply a blockage. By the time I got to the hospital I was close to passing out.

The lads tried their hardest to explain what was wrong with me, but the doctors' broken English made

communication difficult and they just thought I was
very drunk. I was, of course, but they hadn't taken
into consideration this huge lump in my throat. The
next thing I remember was a doctor sticking a needle
in my arm which I think they said was adrenaline,
and then feeling really relaxed.

It turned out that my throat was severely infected.
The heavy session of drink and drugs had caused me
to have a severe reaction and my glands were actually
strangling me. It's an experience I will never forget. I
remember being very scared. My cousin David, who
had never been involved with the drug scene, gave me
a good talking to and I fell asleep crying in his room.
But it didn't stop me sniffing another line the next day.

The football ended with Chelsea getting beaten and
we all made our way back to England feeling sorry for
ourselves – no one more than me. When I got back to
England, I was really looking forward to seeing
Rachel. I'd missed her, and she was waiting for me at
my friend's flat when I got home. She said I looked
really good with the bit of a tan I had picked up.
Considering I'd been only minutes from dying two
nights before, that compliment was all I needed to put
the previous forty-eight hours firmly behind me.

## Out of Control

Several weeks later I rented a nice little two-bedroom
house facing a park, away from the noise of the town.

Shortly after that, Rachel moved in with me and we started to get our new home looking half-decent. However, I still wasn't finished with the drugs, despite the fact that I now had everything I wanted: a nice house, a great girlfriend and a new job as a labourer on a building site. Things were about to go drastically wrong.

Rachel and I both enjoyed a night out, so we regularly popped down to our local and sat and chatted with the regulars, while having a couple of drinks and a few games of pool. This became more and more frequent and my drug intake began to increase again. That's when it happened.

I went to pick up some coke from a regular dealer I knew and was told he had run out, but that he did have some 'stones' (crack cocaine). I agreed to buy a £20 stone, and borrowed his pipe to take this drug.

Being extremely addictive and a lot stronger than normal cocaine, it was no surprise that this stuff blew my head off. The buzz from that first hit was so great that I never wanted to go back to ordinary coke again. Little did I know at the time but my drug habit had just taken a turn for the worse. I started taking crack every other day, and within weeks I'd lost a lot of weight and was looking really ill.

Rachel and I were arguing a lot and I got back into serious debt very quickly. Crack suddenly became my life and everything and everyone else came second. If I couldn't get a stone, I'd drive myself crazy trying. It was such an intense high and such an extreme low, coming down, that I'd do anything I could to stay up.

My paranoia came back with a vengeance and was so extreme that I would go for days without sleep, terrified that I would somehow be killed. I became convinced that there was a hit out on me. My life became completely controlled by this drug and I went downhill rapidly. Words will never be able to explain exactly how bad I was and how close I was to dying. I was having severe panic attacks, I was desperate and scared. I never imagined a few months earlier that my life could get so out of control. I'd search my house from top to bottom for bugs or hidden cameras, convinced that someone was watching me. I'd often cut up my clothes, thinking I could feel a bug in the seam of my jeans or coat. I came very close to cutting myself open, believing that somehow a device had been inserted into my body and it was going to kill me. I started 'seeing things' and hearing voices telling me to do things. I had no relief, no matter what I did or where I went. I was having a complete breakdown mentally, and was close to suicide.

One night I walked over to the motorway bridge near my house and watched the cars and lorries zooming past down below. Convincing myself that it would be best for everyone, including myself, if I ended my life and put an end to this torment, I leant over the railings. There was no other way out that I could see. I felt like my future was a long, dark, empty tunnel. I had no willpower and I certainly didn't have any strength left to fight the thoughts. I had turned from the cockily confident, loud-mouthed drug dealer into a paranoid eight-stone crack cocaine addict with serious mental problems. I was now drowning in thousands of pounds of debt and had thrown away any chance of happiness or future with Rachel, because of the mess I had made of everything. Life appeared to be completely hopeless and jumping in front of a lorry seemed like the most sensible thing to do.

I stared wide-eyed at the speeding traffic whilst wrestling with overwhelming thoughts of death. My brain felt clogged up and crowded, but despite being continuously bombarded by insane thoughts, I knew I couldn't go through with it. I took a step back, then turned and ran to my house and slammed the door behind me.

Once home, the paranoia continued and I spent the next few hours repeatedly searching the house and peeping obsessively out of the windows. After several emotional hours, the drugs finally wore off and, exhausted both mentally and physically, I collapsed on the sofa and fell asleep. Unfortunately this wasn't to be a one-off – the chain of events was repeated the following day, with me once again standing on the bridge contemplating putting an end to it all.

Another night, I was alone in my house after a heavy session on the crack pipe. I had never been so frightened in all my life; the paranoia had completely taken hold of me. I lay curled up in a ball, unable to move, paralysed with fear. As I lay on the floor cold and lonely, petrified and desperate, I heard someone in the room laughing out loud at me. But this was no ordinary laugh. It was a terrifyingly intense, sadistic, haunting cackle that terrified me. I shook with fear. This was different to all the other panic attacks I'd had. I knew that there was no one in my house, and I knew that the laugh wasn't a person. This was the devil. Yes, I was crazy, but this time I wasn't imagining it. I heard the laugh audibly, followed by the chilling words, 'Look what I have reduced you to.' He was enjoying every minute of the misery and torment that I was going through. As I lay there, it felt as if I was under his control. I was at the mercy of the devil, and I was finding out the hard way that there is no mercy in him.

## Ray of Hope

During this time of despair I managed to find a small ray of hope for a short time, when I was invited to spend a week or two with a couple called Freddie and Meg. They were both ex-crack addicts who had turned their lives around after finding God. I knew them both from their drug days and had even spent a night out with Freddie a couple of years previously, taking loads of drugs. I was amazed by the transformation in these two and started to believe that if they could do it, so could I.

They let me stay in their family home with them and their two children, fed me every day and helped me when I was craving drugs. I felt really peaceful whenever I was in their house away from all my problems. I would have loved to stay with them permanently, but I couldn't. They had a family and needed their space. They did, however, help me as much as they could and encouraged me to give my life to Jesus, whom they said would give me his strength to overcome the drugs and the other issues in my life.

The idea of being a Christian still scared me. All I wanted was to be able to give up the drugs, or at least cut down, be able to enjoy a drink in the pub with my mates now and then, and get back with Rachel. There must be a way, I thought. And then something happened that gave me the motivation I had been looking for.

Rachel rang me to say she was going to do a pregnancy test, as it looked as if she might be expecting a baby. When I heard the news that it was positive, my heart started racing. I cried my eyes out as I told Meg, and we both jumped up and down, rejoicing. I'd wanted to be a dad for as long as I could remember. I loved children and convinced myself that this was my last chance, not only to give up drugs but also to get back with Rachel and have the family I'd always wanted.

My head was up in the clouds for a good few weeks and life was great. Rachel and I got back together and were living in the house that belonged to me and my mum. I'd blown over a quarter of a million pounds on drugs since my dad had died, and my half of this house was all I had left.

We had a small room, a shared kitchen and a shower – and that suited us just fine. I signed on with an agency and very quickly found work in a factory. The wages were low but it felt good knowing I was working towards providing for our baby. I also started weight training again. I had always felt more self-confident and secure with a bit of muscle on me. But I wasn't the only one growing. Rachel was getting bigger and bigger every day. I enjoyed nothing more than coming home from work and talking to 'the bump'. We decided that we couldn't wait until the baby was born to find out whether we were going to have a boy or a girl, and so at the second scan we asked the doctor. Something inside me really wanted a little boy. My mum was already sure that it was a boy – God had told her, she said, and she was convinced. The feeling I had when they confirmed that we were indeed going to have a boy was indescribable. I went out of the little room where they did the scans and told my mum, who was waiting outside. We all cried. I felt my life was on the up – as if nothing and no one could take away this natural high I was on. But I was wrong.

## One Last Go

I don't know when exactly it happened or even why, but before long I started having cravings for crack again. I was OK whenever I was around Rachel, but when I was at work, my thoughts would wander, and if

I heard someone so much as talk about drugs, it would plant a seed in my mind that grew very quickly into a full-blown craving. I managed to fight it for a while, but eventually I gave in. I tried to convince myself that I would just have one last go before the baby arrived. And then 'one last go' turned into another 'one last go'. Before I knew it, I was back on crack again full time. I tried my best to cover it up and hide it from Rachel, and tried to convince myself that I could stop before my boy was born. But I was soon caught out.

As I watched Rachel, completely devastated, pack her bags and walk out of the door yet again, I cried and cried. I really didn't want to keep hurting her or anyone else; I hated the way I was, and I'd really tried that time. Suddenly I became very scared for my son's future. How could I raise a little boy while I was still a junkie? How could I get off the drugs and stay off them for good? How was I ever going to make any sort of life for myself and my family? I remembered that evil laugh: 'Look what I have reduced you to.' How could I be free from the demons that had reduced me to this?

# 9

# Good News and Bad News

I'll never forget the day that Rachel walked into my little bedroom and said that she wanted to help me sort myself out. She only had six weeks left before the birth and she'd been spending a lot of time with Nichola, at her house.

Rachel had never stopped loving me. She had left me because she had to do what was right for her and our unborn son. My sister had made her realize that none of this was her fault and it wasn't about me trying to hurt her; it was simply that I was addicted and very, very lost. Rachel told me that not only did she always feel peaceful around my sister, but that she believed that Nichola was right and that the only way I could ever be free from my demons was by allowing Jesus into my life and letting him heal me.

## New Start

I phoned my mum to find out what I had to do to become a true Christian and live the sort of life that she and my sisters did. Right there and then, I dropped to my knees and cried out to God. I was desperate and prayed the prayer mum told me I should pray, inviting Jesus to come into my heart and set me free. I asked him to forgive me for all the terrible things that I could remember doing, and even the things I couldn't. I asked him to give me his strength to stay away from the whole way of life that I had grown up around, not just the drugs. After I had said the prayer, I made a conscious decision to surrender my life to God, and let him do whatever he wanted to with it. Somehow, I just knew God had heard me.

I felt totally different when I woke up the next day. I no longer had the desire to touch any drugs or even to go down the pub. I just felt peace. I remember walking down the road and looking up at the sky, the world around me and at the people walking past me. It was as if my eyes had been opened for the first time in my life – like someone had switched a light on inside me. I knew that God had to have created all this, and that if he created it, he could change it.

I began to feel love for other people – this was totally foreign to me. I knew it was love because it was the opposite of the feelings of anger and hate I was familiar with and had felt whenever I'd looked at people before. I'd been 'born again', as I was to discover the Bible calls it, and now had a brand new view of life. I had a future and a hope.

I arranged to meet up with Mike and Pete, the guys who I'd met at my sister's that day. They were actually a lot calmer than I remembered; I could now see how loving they were and I really felt safe with them. I could tell that they were genuine when they said they wanted to help me get my life back on track.

Once a week at Mike's house a small group got together to pray and read the Bible. I started to go to this meeting, and I loved it. There was Mike, Pete, Mike's son, Ryan, and me. Mike, who was the church pastor, normally shared a message from the Bible and encouraged us in our walk with God. It was at these meetings that I came to see that being a Christian was not just about praying one prayer and asking for forgiveness – it was a journey. And like every journey, you sometimes take the wrong turning or, even worse, crash and end up in a ditch somewhere. I learnt over a period of time that God is always faithful; when I've 'crashed' he has always picked me straight back up and taught me how to overcome the struggles in my life.

## New Life

I can remember every detail of 21 October 2005 as if it were yesterday. It was the early hours of the morning and Rachel and I (who were now back together again)

were at home in bed asleep, when I was woken by
Rachel poking me in the side telling me to wake up.
She was very excited; she told me that her waters had
just broken. In my sleepiness I think I told her she
should have gone to the toilet, but then I realized
what she meant and jumped out of bed. She wasn't in
any pain and we were both unsure about whether she
actually was in labour or not. I decided it was time to
test my new faith, so I closed my eyes and asked God
to let us know what we should do. Within minutes my
mobile phone was ringing. It was five in the morning
and I wasn't expecting any calls. I answered it and
there on the other end of the line was my mum. She'd
woken at the same time as we had, and God had told
her that Rachel was in labour and that she should call
me. She said that we should go straight to the hospital. I cried as she told me, and as we were speaking I
felt this amazing love come over me, not just for the
baby we were about to have, but at the fact that God
had done this. It really broke me.

As calmly as I could, I got together Rachel's hospital
bag and other stuff I thought we might need, and we
waited for Rachel's mum to come and take us to the hospital. I had always thought that women made a bit of a
song and dance about the whole 'giving birth' thing, but
my opinion soon changed when I witnessed what Rachel
went through. She was in labour for thirty hours. I have
never in my life seen such bravery – she was wonderful!

The following day, 22 October, at about 11 a.m. our
son, Callum, was born. He weighed 7lb 15½oz, and he

was gorgeous. When the midwife passed him to me I cried my eyes out. I was so emotionally and physic-ally exhausted that I had to pass him back as I was scared of dropping him. They cleaned him up and put him in a little cot while I ran out to tell all the family, who were waiting in the corridor outside. I could hardly get my words out for crying as I told them all about my very own and very special little man.

We took Callum home not long after that, and once the commotion had died down and everyone else had left us to it I remember thinking, *Life can't get any bet-ter*. I spent hours just looking at him while he slept, and the slightest noise or movement from his Moses basket would have me out of bed and on full alert. He was and still is my pride and joy.

Being a dad was an amazing feeling. I was so proud when I was pushing him down the road in his buggy. I hoped to bump into people I knew and show him off.

As the weeks went by, Callum grew, and so did my faith. I'd started to really see the power of God, and many answers to prayer – far too many for it to be a coincidence. Rachel and I were excited every time God answered one of our needs, and we began to see the love that God has for his children.

We both regularly attended Pastor Mike's church, which he ran with his wife, Heather. It was a small gathering but everyone was very supportive, and I never felt judged because of my past. They all prayed with us and helped out practically when they could.

One of the first major prayers that God answered for us was about our house. We were on a waiting list with the council and had been told we could be waiting for a long time. But it wasn't long at all before we were signing the papers for a nice two-bedroom house not far from the town, with everything we needed. The house needed a lot of work doing to it, but I relished the challenge. I'd go off to work all day, then spend a few hours each night at the new house stripping wallpaper and preparing the rooms for painting. Rachel was very busy looking after Callum, and for a few weeks we spent very little time together. But with some help from friends and family, the house was finally ready to move into, and the three of us were ready to start a new life.

Shortly after we had settled in, I decided I wanted to make things official between us, so I took Rachel for a meal at a nice little Italian restaurant. I had been in earlier in the day to book a table, and had asked the waiter to put a rose in water for when we arrived. I gave him a CD with 'our song' on it and asked him if he would play it when I gave him the nod.

I was very nervous when we sat down to order our food. Rachel had an idea that I was going to propose at some point, because we had been discussing marriage quite a lot, but I was still shaking. Once I had given the nod for our song to be played, I went down on one knee and asked her. I thought I wasn't going to be able to get back up again, I was so shaky, especially with the now busy restaurant, including all the waiters, clapping and cheering as Rachel said, 'Yes.' But I did manage to, and we had a really nice meal and discussed the wedding and how we could make it Rachel's dream day.

## If I'm in the Mud I May as Well Get Dirty

In these first few months of my walk with God, I made more mistakes than I care to remember and one of them nearly cost me everything.

Plans for the wedding started off really well, but then our faith began to get tested. I tried my hardest to be a good Christian, but with the stress of setting up a new home, preparing for a wedding and looking after a new baby, I became increasingly short-tempered and we frequently ended up rowing. I needed a way to let off some steam, and I thought it would be a good idea to join a gym again. Also, I thought it would give me some time to myself a couple of nights a week after work. But soon I was training every day and becoming so wrapped up in it that I was beginning to neglect my duties as a dad and as a partner.

I was working really hard at the building site, and I had even been put in charge of about six blokes. After work I went to the gym for an hour or so, before coming home for my dinner and a rest. By the time I had played with Callum and sat down for half an hour I was far too tired to pray, let alone read my Bible. Very soon I made the biggest mistake of my life.

I wasn't happy with the weights I was lifting, because I had lifted much heavier ones before. Of course, that was when I was on steroids, but it still annoyed me and I started to entertain thoughts of doing a quick course of them to help me blow up a bit again. It started with a small amount here and there. I promised myself that I would restrict the amount I took, but I should have known better. Within a few weeks I was jabbing needles in myself every other day and popping the strongest form of oral steroids you could get.

Rachel was no fool – she remembered the way that my body changed the last time I used steroids, and she began asking questions. I knew lying was wrong by now, but I did it anyway and often swore to her that I wasn't taking anything. One lie led to another lie to cover up the last one, and before I knew it, I was acting just like the old me.

Friends regularly reminded me about the importance of daily Bible reading and spending time talking to God, but I was neglecting all of that and it started to show. I gradually started to find myself craving a night out again, and the idea of drugs kept entering my head. While I had been regularly praying and studying the Bible I had never once had those temptations, and I learnt the hard way that you reap what you sow. I crashed in a major way.

I've since learnt by experience that if you keep giving God your time and he sees that you are willing to change, he will change you. Unfortunately, I wasn't listening to the good advice that I was being given by wise Christians friends.

And so I gave in to the temptation of a night out with a few of my old friends, and soon found myself half-drunk and feeling really wound up. I'd had a few vodkas, but that was no excuse for what I did. A guy on the dance floor kept bumping into two of the girls I was with. He didn't listen to my warning so, without even thinking, I head-butted him and had him thrown out of the pub. There I was on the dance floor, drunk and about to kick off with the bouncers. What sort of Christian was I? My attitude then was, 'If I'm in the mud I may as well get dirty,' and on the journey home, as we sped down the motorway, I used a coin to scoop some coke out of a small bag and stick it up my nose. I knew I was making a huge mistake, but I still went ahead with it, and it led to a two-day session.

Understandably, Rachel went crazy and wanted me out of the house. The wedding was called off, and so was our relationship. Now I had two options running through my head: either go back to that old, familiar but miserable life of drink and drugs or cry out to God and ask for forgiveness and strength. Thankfully, I took the second option and ran straight back to God.

Pastor Mike, Pete and Ryan, as well as my family, walked me through it again and helped me back onto my feet. They explained to me that just because we are Christians it doesn't mean we are invincible. As real as God is, so is the devil and he will always do what he can to trip us up. The Bible tells us that the only thing the devil does is steal, kill and destroy our lives. But God in his mercy and unfailing love for us has, by his Holy Spirit, enabled us to overcome the devil.

Rachel and I never got back together again. As I have learnt, sin has consequences. We may be forgiven and God doesn't treat us as our sins deserve, but often we still have to live with the consequences of our actions. God is righteous and just. Thanks to him I still have a very good friendship with Rachel and a fantastic relationship with my son. Rachel says she is really pleased because she has seen my life change so radically.

## Encounter

Some time after all this, I went away for a weekend 'encounter' with my church. Basically, this was a short trip with other Christians to different surroundings, away from distractions, into an environment that allows you the chance to forget about regular nine-to-five living and meet God in a personal way. I loved it – the worship music, the teaching and the prayer. I developed a real passion for prayer, especially once I discovered that God actually does talk back!

Pastor Mike had explained to me all about the Holy Spirit: how, when we are filled with him it gives us a new strength and he empowers us to do things we could never do in the natural. He showed me the bit in the book of Acts, chapter 1, verse 8, where it tells us that the Holy Spirit will come on us and give us power. This is exactly how it was for me when Pastor Mike prayed for me to receive the Holy Spirit. In Acts chapter 2, verse 4 it says that as they were filled with the Holy Spirit they began to speak different languages, sometimes known as 'tongues'.

I had overheard my mum praying in the past, and quite often it was in this language I couldn't understand. I regularly accused her of being 'a sandwich short of a picnic', but all of a sudden, as Mike prayed, it happened to me – I started speaking in a language I didn't know. Not just that, but I couldn't stop. I had absolutely no idea what I was saying, but I knew it was from God. As it was happening, I began to weep as I felt love and joy wash over me like nothing I had ever felt before. I am still so grateful to God for blessing me with this wonderful gift.

However, the fact that I had been filled with the Holy Spirit and was walking with God didn't mean that everything would be plain sailing from now on and all my struggles were over. I discovered that the choices we make can continue to have a huge effect on us later in life. In fact, not just the choices we make, but often the choices our parents make, have a lasting effect on the course of our lives. Still, whenever I am feeling low, or when things are getting to me, I cry out to God in this language and feel his peace come straight back to me. He is faithful, even when I'm not. He always picks me up, dusts me off, and puts me back on the right path.

# 10

# New Horizons

After the slip-up that cost me so much, I was totally broken. But I saw the love of God practically demonstrated by Christian friends. Mike and Heather were fantastic – every time I fell on my face, God used them to pick me back up. I'll never be able to fully express what they did for me and do them justice. The love they showed me could only have come from God, and I am so grateful to them for the way they pastored me. I truly believe that they saved my life by introducing me to the life that they have been living for many years now. They never spoke a negative word to me, and despite the amount of times I let them down by throwing their help back in their faces and ignoring the advice that they so freely offered, they always welcomed me back into their house, prayed for me and nurtured me through some of the most difficult periods. They taught me the foundations that I needed to get through those tough times. When they humbly felt they couldn't take me any further as pastors, they encouraged me to move on to a bigger church, suggesting one in Newcastle they knew of.

So I decided to visit this church in Newcastle. I'd never been to Newcastle before and had no idea about this church other than what I had heard from Pastor Mike. My friend Ryan was already there staying with a family he knew, and they offered to let me go up and stay for a weekend. I packed a bag and got on the train heading north, not having any idea at all of what I was going to do or even what to expect. But the church was great and, as well as the church itself, they also had the 24-hour House of Prayer (HOP) in Sunderland, which was the most amazing place I had ever seen.

The first time I walked into the HOP, I felt the awesome presence of God and fell in love with the place. That first time I visited, I was sitting talking with Ryan and we were praying together about our very different situations, when God spoke quite clearly to us both. I had just received a phone call from Rachel giving me her answer about whether we should give our relationship one last try or not. Her answer had come back: 'No.' I was devastated, but only had myself to blame. I remember having many different emotions as I sat at a table in the HOP considering my future. I looked around at the new surroundings and started to feel that maybe God was telling me I should move up to Newcastle for a while to get my life back on track and become more secure and grounded in God. Whilst I was praying about it, a man came over and confirmed this to me by a word of prophecy (a word given to him by God – also a gift of the Holy Spirit). I knew it was right, and also knew I had to act on this word immediately.

## Moving North

I went home, collected my things, said goodbye to my little boy and made plans to catch the next available train back to Newcastle to begin a new life up north. It was one of the hardest decisions I have ever made and one I took very seriously. As I lay in bed the night before I was due to move, I remember debating whether or not I was making the right decision. I told God that unless he confirmed very clearly that it was right, I wasn't going to go. He then spoke to me by leading me to read the book of Romans, chapter 5, verses 3, 4 and 5. It says that we are to rejoice in our troubles, as they make us more patient, strengthen our character, and give us hope. In those three verses I heard God confirm to me that although I was going to suffer by being away from my son and my family, it was going to produce character in me, and hope. I fell asleep with all the peace I needed, knowing that although it was going to be hard, I had to trust God. I knew that if I was ever going to be totally free from my struggles and be the sort of dad that Callum deserved, I had to take some time to let God work on me and heal me.

The next day I nervously boarded the train. Whilst I was travelling, I spent the entire three hours reading a book called *Run Baby Run* by a man named Nicky Cruz. This guy was an ex-New York gang leader. He had been the most feared member of the Mau Maus, a ruthless gang that were involved in drugs, violence and even murder. This guy told his story of hell on earth and how his life changed dramatically when he found the love of God and was set free. Reading this book was a real encouragement to me – if God did it for Nicky, he could do it for me, and I was looking forward to finding out just how much God could change my life.

Just before I arrived at Newcastle train station, I told God that if he was indeed leading me to this city, then he would have to provide everything I needed. I'd already been offered a place to stay, but I would need a job ASAP to keep me there. I also asked for enough money to enable me to provide for my son and to pay off the debts that I still had from my drug days.

God didn't disappoint me, and within three days I had a good job within walking distance from where I was staying, and enough of a wage to keep me as well as send money home for Callum each week.

After I had been in Newcastle for about a week, I went to one of the church's Friday night meetings in Sunderland. It was amazing. I had a great time and got to know loads of people. They really welcomed me and made me feel at home. I really felt and knew that I 'belonged' and that felt good. When the meeting finished, I chatted for a while to some of the guys. Several of them were going back to someone's home for pizza and to hang out, but I had the feeling that I should stay at the church overnight. I kept trying to fight it, but every time I tried to leave I couldn't. I spoke to a guy about it and he told me to read the book of 1 Samuel. The bit in chapter 3 where Samuel sleeps in the temple jumped out at me, and I knew that God wanted me to stay in the House of Prayer.

I found a place to pray and started talking to God, but I felt that he was telling me to just rest. It was as if he wanted to do something for me and he just wanted me to sleep while he did it. The next morning I woke early and didn't feel much different. I thought maybe I had heard wrong. Perhaps I was making it all up in my head. *Oh well*, I thought, *while I'm here I may as well read my Bible for a bit, and then go home.* And that was when it happened. As I read my Bible I began to cry and cry and cry. The strange thing was, I wasn't feeling sad. In fact far from it, so why was I crying? And then I heard God's voice clearly in my head. He said to me, 'You are free.' I looked down and immediately saw the word 'free' in my Bible. It was as if my eyes couldn't leave that word. Then again I heard him say to me clearly, 'While you were asleep, I removed the addictions.' And I literally did feel it.

I ran to the altar of the church and cried for ages while thanking God for what he had done for me. I saw that there had been a huge generational curse of addiction on my family, and God had broken it. Many members of my family had been alcoholics, and by the time the curse was in my life, it had progressed to drugs. But all that was over now. One touch from God and my life was never to be the same again.

God had removed the addiction that had held me captive over the past ten years of my life, and now he was starting to add things as well. I've learnt that God never removes something without also replacing it with something good. Each time I have been obedient in getting rid of something that he has asked me to, he has been faithful in replacing it with something far greater, purer and better. Many people resist the work of God in their lives because they believe him to be a strict master who will spoil all their fun, but I have learnt that he is not like that and only removes the things that he is wise enough to know will damage our lives and prevent us from fulfilling the potential that he has placed inside of each of us.

## Laying Strong Foundations

I spent about four years living in the north-east of England and applied myself diligently to learning more about the Bible and about God and what he is really like. I travelled back down south twice a month to start with, to visit my son Callum, and was always amazed at how much he had grown and changed. Being away from him was the hardest part of this time for me. I often cried. I felt extremely guilty for having left him and missed him terribly. But I knew that going to Newcastle was the right thing to do to enable me to become grounded and strengthened in my faith, away from all the old temptations. I desperately wanted to be a good dad to Callum – one who was free of all addiction, anger and insecurity, so that I could eventually return to him and be the father he deserved.

I began to miss him so much that I started making the four-hour journey every week just to spend half a day with my special little boy, and the desire to be back with him was so strong.

By now, though, I had started preaching quite a bit at events across the UK and was doing some ministry in the local schools. I was developing a real passion for seeing broken lives restored back to the amazing God I had encountered and grown to love so much. There was even talk of me pastoring a local church and becoming a leader in the north-east, but I knew that God wanted me back near my son.

I had come to the conclusion, after much heart-searching and prayer, that Rachel was not to be my wife after all, and I began to feel a new kind of love for her, that of a good friend. However, I did desire to be married to a good Christian woman who loved Jesus – and could sing. I always had loved women who could sing, and so I prayed and searched for this woman to share my new life and passion with. Sadly I made many mistakes in this area, and noticed some real issues in my heart that needed dealing with before I could seriously entertain the idea of marriage. I spent a lot of time going through counselling and dealing with wrong mindsets and attitudes, but I was diligent in this as I recognized that I needed to be free of all the negative aspects of my past life.

I eventually founded my own charity called 'Storming the Nations' and started going into schools, prisons, churches and a variety of events to share God's transforming love and power with as many people as I could. Invitations began to come in from different parts of the country and I developed a real passion for preaching the Bible.

Despite all the good things that were developing in my life, there was still one area of my past life that I could not seem to break free from – pornography. It was not something I looked at every day, or even every week, but it did seem to have a vice-like grip on my heart and left me feeling very dirty and ashamed. Before I became a Christian I hadn't seen anything wrong with viewing this kind of material, but now I felt . . . not just felt, I knew that it was wrong and desperately wanted to stop looking at it. I prayed a lot, cried a lot and spoke to many of my Christian friends and leaders about it, yet still I was not free. I even contemplated giving up the work I knew God had given to me, as I felt unworthy.

# Lydia

One day I was due to share my testimony and speak to young people about Jesus at a special event in Royston, which was near my old home town. I was excited, as always, to be speaking, and drove down to be a part of this Easter event. When I arrived, I made my way into the main hall and noticed several people setting up ready for the day. It was then that I saw her – Lydia, one of the singers in the band. She seemed really shy and I couldn't help but notice her.

The day was a tremendous success and 32 young people made decisions to become Christians. Some of them were physically healed and began to weep. It was incredible.

Afterwards I spoke a little to Lydia and we later became friends on Facebook. Then we arranged to go out together and started dating. It was not long before we fell in love and started talking about marriage, and she was planning to join me up north and help me with the ministry.

However, my heart still longed for my son. Did I really have to stay so far away from him? One night I was praying and felt that it was now the right time to move back down south and be a part of his life. But I was determined not to move unless it was the will of God. Lydia was spending nine months in America at a worship training school. When I told her about my desire to live in the south of England, near my son, her response was so encouraging. She told me that she would go wherever I went and support me no matter what. During this very difficult time of decision-making I was feeling very stressed and confused, but thankfully God spoke to someone on our behalf which confirmed that this was the right decision. A man walked up to Lydia in America and told her that he had a prophetic word from God for us both. As it was very directional he was a little nervous about sharing it. This was the word: 'God is telling you and Rob to stay south. Do not move north.'

Lydia and I married in August 2010 and we moved into a lovely little cottage which was about twenty minutes from where my son lived and went to school. We joined a thriving local church. Lydia soon joined the worship team and I became a member of the church staff in the role of evangelist, preaching every Sunday night and taking teams out to the streets – my old streets! I began to pick my son up from school twice a week, and he started to stay overnight and every other weekend, coming to church and getting involved in everything.

Today, Lydia and I are good friends with Rachel and sometimes we all take Callum out together, so he knows that there is restoration. God has worked amazingly in Rachel's heart, and she has been able to forgive me for what I put her through. I have apologized to many of the people I hurt over the years. My old gang friends often contact me for prayer and advice, and some of them have changed their lives, too.

Lydia and I now travel up and down the country, sharing Jesus. So I've got a beautiful wife, who has an amazing singing ministry and is part of a great band called The Heritage. We love the itinerant lifestyle and get to serve God together. We have seen powerful miracles time and time again, proving that God is real, and not only is he real, but he is in the business of transforming anyone who will surrender their life to him.

## 11

# A Work in Progress

I've seen God do so many incredible things in my heart and mind since I became a Christian on 11 September 2005. He really has radically transformed my life. I am now unrecognizable from the old Rob Joy you have been reading about. My entire way of thinking is different; I hate violence, and I am completely free of addiction. Despite several mistakes and slip-ups, God refused to let me go and he patiently and faithfully went to work, changing me and delivering me from so much of my past. However, I still had to make some very important and crucial life decisions in order to move forward in my new faith and life in Christ.

Being a Christian isn't easy. We face the same struggles, the same problems and the same pain that everyone else does, but the difference is that we have an amazing Father in heaven who wants to guide us through and help us to live the way he always intended us to live, having a relationship with him.

I'm not just telling you what it says in the Bible, I'm talking from experience. I used to have so many arguments against God, but over time he has demonstrated to me just how real he is and how he is more than capable of changing any situation. But he will not force himself on us; we need to let him help us and trust him.

## Trust Him

Trusting God and letting him have control of our lives is the key. God has given us all free will, and it's something he'll never take from us, even if it means we make wrong choices. When I first became a Christian, Proverbs chapter 3, verses 5 and 6 were very important to me. These verses say, 'Trust the LORD completely, and don't depend on your own knowledge. With every step you take, think about what he wants, and he will help you go the right way.' Although God helps us go the right way, because we have free will we can choose, at any time, to wander off in the other direction – and, like a complete fool, I did that on a number of occasions. The Bible also says in 1 Peter chapter 5, verse 5 that 'God is against the proud, but he is kind to the humble.' We need to put our pride to one side and admit that we can't do it alone and that we need God and his word, the Bible, to survive. We need to allow him to help us.

## Let Go and Let God

One of the my favourite books in the Bible is the Gospel of Matthew. It really shows us the heart and character of Jesus Christ. In Matthew chapter 10, verse 39 Jesus says, 'Those who try to keep the life they have will lose it. But those who give up their life for me will find true life.' So many people, me included, have things in their lives that they just don't want to let go of. They're not prepared to lose that thing – in fact, even the thought of giving it up terrifies them. They've either grown attached to it or, worse still, they have become dependent upon it. (That 'thing' might also be a person.) I was dependent on a lot of things, not just drugs. But as the verse above says – and I have learnt by experience – if we are prepared to let those things go and completely trust God, he will make our lives more fulfilling than we could ever imagine.

When we decide to give up everything and follow God, he'll bless us, satisfy us and provide for our every need. It says in the Bible that if we put God first and what he wants, he'll take care of everything else (check out Matthew's Gospel chapter 6, verse 33). Most people have it mixed up. They seek life and the things it offers and completely ignore God. At the end of the day, when you realize that not only did he create the heavens and the earth but also everything in it, including you, then you'll realize he's much better qualified than you are to know what you do and do not need. The reason I was scared to hand over control of my life to God and trust him was because I liked some things I knew he didn't. But as I have said before, God never takes something away without replacing it with something much better. And, thankfully, he doesn't do the removing all at once. It's an ongoing process that he does at a rate he knows we can cope with.

If you were to ask any good father what he wants for his children, it would be the best possible life – great education, great job, amazing family, happiness and so on. It's natural. But as a dad, I also know what it's like to have your child rebel and ignore your advice. When kids are naughty it upsets the parent, but it never stops them loving them. It's the same for God. He has to watch his children repeatedly mess up, fall over and do things that really upset him, but he never stops loving them. Ever! All he wants is for us to stop running and say, 'OK, Dad, I'm sorry. I tried it my way and I got in loads of trouble. Will you forgive me and take this huge mess I've made of my life and fix it for me?' It's as simple as that.

## God Loves You

God created us and loves us, his children. He created us with free will but, sadly, right from the start, with Adam and Eve, we chose to rebel rather than live God's way and so walked away from that relationship with him. Every single one of us sins and does bad things. However, God is completely good and can't have a relationship with anything evil. He wants our relationship with him to be restored, but to do that we need to become sinless. We are unable to do it by ourselves, so God has made a way. He sent his son Jesus to earth to live as a perfect man, completely without sin. He then allowed him, though he was innocent of any crime, to be put to death on a cross to take the punishment for all our sin. This means if we come to God and ask for forgiveness, and acknowledge that Jesus has taken our punishment for us, our slate is wiped clean, we are considered sinless in the sight of God. This enables us to have the relationship with him that he has always desired, and which will continue for eternity. Jesus took the punishment once and for all, for all the bad stuff we've ever done or will do when he died; he took the punishment we deserve so we could be free of it. All we have to do is admit our sin and surrender our lives to God.

If you're prepared to surrender your life to God and admit to him that whatever your life's like at the moment, good or bad, it could still be much better and, more importantly, acknowledge that Jesus died to take the punishment for your sins, give you eternal life and set you free, I encourage you to pray the following prayer out loud. If you're willing to trust your life to him so that he can give it back to you with so much more than you could possibly imagine, then say the following prayer:

Dear God

I now recognize that what the Bible says is true, and that you really do love me. So much so, that you were willing to send your only son, Jesus, to die on a cross, to pay the penalty for every sin I have committed against you. I am so sorry for the way I've lived my life up until now, doing what I wanted. Please forgive me and help me to do what is right. Father, I receive your free and amazing gift of eternal life and I invite you to enter my heart and teach me your ways for-ever.

In Jesus' name

Amen

If you have just said that prayer, then I would love to hear from you and find out more. My email address is at the end of the book.

One of the things that I have found from personal expe-rience to be very important is finding a good church to be part of, where you can be loved and challenged. Ask God to direct you to the church he wants you to join, and he will. I pray that you will grow in faith as you walk with God and that you, like me, will come to see how amazing and life-changing having a relationship with God really is. You only have one life, so why waste it? Let God fulfil you and heal you from the inside out.

If you didn't say that prayer but would still like to know more, or feel that perhaps God was speaking to you through this book but are unsure, confused or maybe just have some questions, then please feel free to contact me. I don't have all the answers, but I do know God does. Since meeting him my life has never been the same. God can touch you in the very same way as he did me – a real way. Simply surrender. Surrender to him and I guarantee that not only will you find the truth, but . . .

## THE TRUTH WILL SET YOU FREE

I would love to hear from you if you have any
questions or need prayer or support.
You can contact me by email at

**robjoy911@yahoo.co.uk**

Follow me on **Twitter: rob_joy**

**Storming the Nations**

We have a monthly newsletter that you can sign up
to, and you can receive regular updates, itinerary
and news by visiting our website
**www.stormingthenations.net**
**www.theheritage.org.uk**

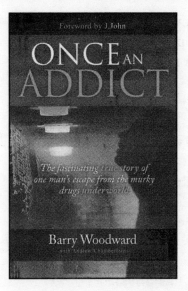

## Once an Addict

*The Fascinating True Story of One Man's Escape from the Murky Drugs Underworld*

*Barry Woodward*
*with Andrew Chamberlain*

Barry Woodward was a drug dealer and heroin addict who once lived on the notorious Bull Rings in the centre of Manchester. *Once an Addict* describes Barry's descent into the murky underworld of drug dealing, addiction, crime and imprisonment. Along the way we are introduced to some of the most extraordinary characters, and we see the extreme lengths to which some of them will go to get their next 'fix'. Illegal drug use claimed the lives of many such people, and it seemed inevitable that Barry would also succumb to the consequences of his addiction.

With devastating amphetamine-induced mental health issues, a fourteen-year heroin addiction, a string of broken relationships, and the threat of HIV looming, the outlook for Barry appeared very bleak. Then three extraordinary encounters changed his life forever . . .

**978-1-86024-602-9**

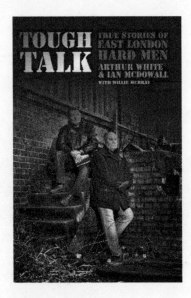

# Tough Talk

### *True Stories of East London Hard Men*

## *Arthur White and Ian McDowall*
### *with Millie Murray*

**Arthur's Story**
World champion powerlifter, successful businessman, happy family man. But Arthur's life spiralled out of control. Cocaine, steroids and an affair ruined everything and he lost his business, family – all the things that were really important. Death seemed the only way out. What changed him?

**Ian's Story**
Body building was Ian's life and he was determined to become No.1 at all costs. Being a doorman and debt collector enabled him to sustain his use of illegal steroids. Cheating in his sport, robbing on the door – Ian's days were filled with violence and deceit. What changed him?

**978-1-86024-823-8**

# Tough Talk 2

*More Life-Changing Stories from the Tough Talk Team*

### *with*
### *Millie Murray*

**Joe Lampshire** – '"YOU WILL DIE" . . . Playing the Ouija board was just for a laugh; I had done it many times before. But this was something way, way out of my experience and it wasn't funny.' For Joe, this was just the beginning of a long battle with the spirit world. As dark forces threatened to claim Joe's life, could light ever break through?

**Martyn Parrish** – 'It was heady stuff and, of course, I wanted to do it again. I wanted to drop some pills and then ride my bike. This was living! Or so I thought.' At first the drugs freed Martyn's mind, and then they began to completely take over. As heroin became Martyn's closest and most destructive friend, could he ever find peace?

**Simon Pinchbeck** – 'I'd been greedy, thinking how much I'd make out of my investment, and now it was gone. I felt the need to settle the matter, preferably by slowly killing each man involved.' A hunger for money and involvement with tough and violent police corps had sent Simon's life spiralling out of control. Deserted by friends and in huge debt, would he ever find a way out?

**978-1-86024-700-2**

# Tough Talk – True Life Stories

*Stories of East London Hard Men, Ex-Bouncers and Debt Collectors*

This DVD tells the incredible stories of Arthur White, Steve Johnson, Ian McDowall and Marcus Williams. Each has a powerful story of how God rescued them from lives of violence, drug abuse and alcoholism.

**5028981021550**

# Stories From the Front Line

*DVD with Study Guide*
*Tough Talk*

Members of the Tough Talk team discuss candidly the topics of pornography, addiction, anger and forgiveness.
The guys don't pretend to have all the answers but talk openly and honestly of their own battles with these issues. The short study guide which comes in the pack provides material for group discussion on each of the topics.

**5014182055197**

# Taming the Tiger

***From the Depths of Hell
to the Heights of Glory
The Remarkable True
Story of a Kung Fu
World Champion***

*Tony Anthony*
*with Angela Little*

Tony Anthony knew no fear. Three-times World Kung Fu Champion, he was self-assured, powerful and at the pinnacle of his art. An extraordinary career awaited him.

This fast-paced, compelling and, at times, chilling account is Tony's deeply moving true story. More extraordinary than fantasy, more remarkable than fiction, this blockbusting read almost defies belief. With fascinating insight into China's martial arts, and the knife-edge adrenaline highs of the bodyguard lifestyle, it documents the personal tragedy that turned a 'disciple of enlightenment' into a bloodthirsty, violent man.

From the depths of hell in Cyprus's notorious Nicosia Central Prison, all might have been lost, but for the visits of a stranger . . .

**978-1-86024-481-0**

# The Power & the Glory

### *The Remarkable Story of a Four-Time World Powerlifting Champion*

## *Arthur White & Martin Saunders*

Arthur White had it all. Not only was he a successful businessman and happy family man, but as a champion powerlifter, he was literally on top of the world. But when he got to the top, he wasn't satisfied . . .

As he searched for a greater high, Arthur's life spiralled out of control. Drug addiction, an intense affair and a descent into violence followed, and before long death seemed like the only way out. As he stared into the abyss, an incredible encounter turned Arthur's life upside down. He would never be the same again . . .

**978-1-86024-560-2**

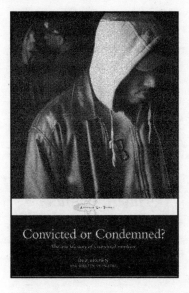

Convicted or Condemned?

The true Mystery of a convicted murderer

DEZ BROWN
with MARTIN SAUNDERS

# Convicted or Condemned?

## The True Life Story of a Convicted Murderer

## Dez Brown
### with Martin Saunders

'I stepped back, turned around and started walking away. From behind me, I heard a shout: "He's stabbed me! He's stabbed me!" I had stabbed him. In one fluid moment, and almost without truly thinking about it, I had drawn my knife and plunged it into his body.'

In an instant, Dez Brown's life had inalterably changed direction. As he unintentionally ended the life of a stranger in a busy London park, Dez dived headlong into a downward spiral that would almost certainly lead to prison and a life in ruins.

A gritty true story, written from the heart, *Convicted or Condemned?* is the sometimes dark but ultimately inspiring story of one man's journey to redemption. What happened next was truly incredible . . .

978-1-86024-484-1

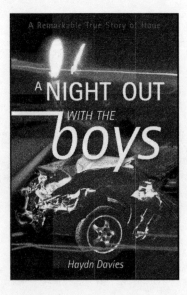

# A Night Out with the Boys

## *A Remarkable True Story of Hope*

### *Haydn Davies*

Haydn was an ordinary lad with an extraordinary gift. Selected for the Welsh under-21 football team at a young age, he had a promising career ahead. Yet all of this disappeared after a sudden car accident. He was propelled into a life of uncertainty, his spinal chord almost severed. Faced with a future of operations and wheelchairs, things looked bleak. But why? Why had this happened? Was it for a reason?

**978-1-85078-735-8**

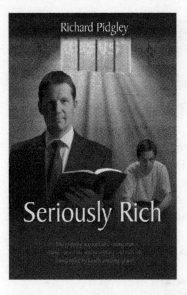

# Seriously Rich

*The Gripping Account of a Young Man Whose Ruined Life was Powerfully and Radically Transformed by God's Amazing Grace!*

*Richard Pidgley*

As a teenager, Richard Pidgley was already well on the way to becoming a career criminal. Life had reached rock bottom and the only way out seemed to be to take his own life . . .

Following the break up of his parents' marriage when he was just 18 months old, Richard spent his early years in a succession of foster and children's homes. Bullied severely and deprived of the love and stability of a normal family, it wasn't long before Richard slid into the criminal world, dabbling in the occult, alcohol abuse, sex and drugs. Arrested and charged for burglary, he was sent to Dorchester Prison where suicide seemed to be the only option. Miraculously he survived, but that was only the beginning. What happened next was truly incredible . . .

**978-1-86024-807-8**

**Authentic**

We trust you enjoyed reading this book from
Authentic Media Limited. If you want to be informed
of any new titles from this author and other exciting
releases you can sign up to the Authentic Book
Club online:

www.authenticmedia.co.uk/bookclub

Contact us
By Post: Authentic Media Limited
52 Presley Way
Crownhill
Milton Keynes
MK8 0ES

E-mail: info@authenticmedia.co.uk

Follow us: